GW00373877

Thomas Strasser

MIND THE APP!

Inspiring internet tools and activities to engage your students

HELBLING LANGUAGES

With website backup

Mind the App!
by Thomas Strasser
© HELBLING LANGUAGES

First published 2012
10 9   8   7   6   5   4   3   2
2017   2016   2015   2014   2013

ISBN 978-3-85272-556-7

Edited by Daniel Martín
Copy-edited by Caroline Petherick and Oonagh Wade
Designed by Pixarte
Cover design by Capolinea
Printed by Athesia

The publisher would like to thank these sources for their kind permission to reproduce screenshots from their websites:
Learning Apps, Quietube, Classtools, mailVU, Wordle, Capzles, PhasR, Photovisi, Storybird, Prezi, Wordsift, Animoto, Screenr, Markup, Crocodoc, TodaysMeet, Popplet, Voicethread, Wallwisher, Voki, Little Bird Tales, Livebinders, Flipsnack, Penzu, Zooburst, Toondoo, Cueprompter.

Every effort has been made to trace the owners of any copyright material in this book. If notified, the publisher will be pleased to rectify any errors or omissions.

Acknowledgements

Thanks to:

Birgit Strasser, my lovely wife, who has always supported this project.
My gorgeous kids, Lisa and Lilly, who made me smile and laugh during work!
Lucia Astuti for offering me the chance to write this book.
Caroline Petherick and Daniel Martín for their great expertise and support.
Prof. Steve Wheeler, Prof. Alec Couros and Nik Peachey for being such vital sources of inspiration.
Günter and Erika Froneberg for giving me valuable feedback.
Silvia Jindra for her idea to present this book to Helbling Languages.
Jürgen Wagner for being a great advisor.

Contents

Contents

Introduction

The buzzword 'Web 2.0' (O'Reilly 2004) has become increasingly popular nowadays. Social networking sites like Twitter or Facebook, and sites such as Wikipedia and YouTube that are rich in content created by users, are now part of many people's everyday lives.

In this book, we are going to help you make full use of Web 2.0. However, it is also important to understand what Web 1.0 was (cf Peachey). Web 1.0 can be seen as the old version of the internet; in general, people used it – as we still do – to surf the net to get information. That information was controlled by a small group of IT specialists or programmers who provided their data. Nearly everything on the internet used to move in a linear, one-way direction. Website content was provided for users to read the news, watch videos or download articles. Until recently, people did not upload anything much to the web, partly because the old internet was very technical (you had to know programming language to create a website), so it was not really interactive at all. Also, internet connections were not fast enough to allow people to upload videos, pictures or music, or to watch videos streaming down their phone line. So, even though people could create email accounts to send and receive emails etc., there was not much room to create content or to interact with content already there.

Web 2.0 is different. There are several definitions of what it is (O'Reilly, Kerres, Alby, etc.) and, although there are a few variations in the perception of Web 2.0, there are certain characteristics that almost all IT experts and educationalists agree on:

The web has become democratic because it is socially connected. You, the user, have the opportunity to take part in the internet. By doing things such as publishing blogs, posting messages on Facebook or Twitter, uploading videos on YouTube and photos on Picasa, Google+Local, and Pinterest, and writing Wikipedia entries, users have become an important part of an interactive World Wide Web without having any IT-related knowledge other than a few basic skills! With a click of the mouse your content can be made available to the world. Now we can truly say 'the net isn't them' and 'the net is us' and 'we are the internet.'

For most of us, there are many advantages to social media and Web 2.0:

- There is no need to buy expensive software any more. The idea behind Web 2.0 is that content can be created, shared and modified with (the mainly free) applications that provide the tools and services to do so.
- An example of how democratic the web has become is that TV programmes can now easily make use of users' material, mainly pictures and video recordings posted on the internet.
- Social networking sites connect and unite people to such an extent that some revolutions would not otherwise have been possible (e.g. Twitter was used to organise demonstrations in Egypt, Libya, etc.).

- Social networking and Web 2.0 can influence voters' behaviour. It could be argued that Barack Obama won the elections in 2008 due to his witty use of social media and Web 2.0 (music videos on YouTube, and his Facebook and Twitter accounts etc.).
- Web 2.0 is rapidly changing the way people – especially the younger generation – interact. Whether this is for better or worse is perhaps uncertain at this stage.
- What is certainly good is that it has created new forms of literacy (e.g. enabling people to produce informative, creative and unique content, critically reflect on sources, improve their IT skills etc.).
- Web 2.0 encourages creativity and supports talent. A lot of people have now got a chance to present their creativity publicly, by performing on YouTube videos or their Facebook page. Many bands and artists have been discovered through their social media channels.

In addition, Web 2.0 follows the gradual introduction around the world of broadband internet connections for surfing that is fun and fast. Due to this and to broadband costs dropping in many places, people can have a wonderfully rich media experience on the web: and, for an increasing number of us, watching clips on YouTube or listening to podcasts is no longer frustrating, because we are getting fast and reliable data transfer.

Web 2.0 is not dependent on software that you have to buy; there is a vast choice of free applications that can be downloaded. Using all these mainly free, user-friendly applications, you can enjoy interacting and sharing material (including pod- or videocasts that you have made yourself) with your chosen audience.

This book aims to provide teachers with a complete introduction to the apps necessary to use and manage content on the web. Each activity has a detailed, illustrated explanation of how to use the app so teachers become thoroughly familiar with it before introducing it to students.

WHY USE WEB 2.0 TOOLS IN THE CLASSROOM?
Web 2.0 is interactive
Social networking sites such as Facebook or Twitter, blogs (Wordpress, Tumblr) and wikis (Wikispaces, Wikipedia) offer you and your students the chance to interact with the community, and indeed with users from all over the world. Imagine you want to know how to fix a problem with your computer, or you want to know where to stay in London; just use your social channels and you can be sure of getting at least some sort of an answer within minutes!

Web 2.0 is creative
Using Web 2.0 applications like Glogster or Animoto, your learners can create interactive and graphically appealing presentations which they can use for their websites and blogs. Since these applications allow them to easily embed various media (songs, videos, images, etc.), their creative potential is well supported.

Web 2.0 is open source

Open source applications are free. They are not sold, like commercial products, but they are freely available – and they are flexible, meaning the users can change the settings (design, functions, etc.).

Since a wide community uses open source applications for free, there is constant retuning, bug fixing (i.e. fixing errors) and feedback, often resulting in programs (like Mozilla's web browser Firefox) that are far better constructed, so are less 'clunky' and far more secure than the commercial alternatives. Several Web 2.0 applications like Classtools (quizzes) or Widgetbox (creating useful gadgets for your blog) help users change layout and content in order to adapt them to their learning needs.

Having said that, do use your common sense when deciding whether or not to reveal personal details to any website - for more guidance on this, see under Concerns on p. 11.

Web 2.0 is collaborative

Mindmapping or text-writing applications like Popplet or PiratePad, plus wikis and blogs, make collaboration between learners easy. By using these tools, learners can share their ideas or write a text together.

Web 2.0 is fast

Networking sites such as Facebook or Twitter guarantee that certain information the learner needs from the teacher and their classmates (content, deadlines, news etc.) is rapidly accessible and shared among the community.

Web 2.0 expands knowledge

Twitter and Facebook are used by many educators to post interesting videos or links for the classroom or to hold debates. In the course of an intensive discussion, input is given and new knowledge is generated.

Web 2.0 provides the target language

The lingua franca on the web is undoubtedly English. By browsing the web and learning how to use the apps and tools available, the students are constantly exposed to the target language in a way they find useful – and enjoy!

Web 2.0 supports digital literacy

When working with Web 2.0 tools, students gain a deeper understanding of technologies (computers, internet and apps in particular). In general, teenagers/young learners are, for the most part, digitally competent or supposed 'digital natives', and can use technologies more effectively. However, they may not be fully aware of certain things such as internet safety, creating secure passwords, copyright issues, creating secondary email accounts. When working with Web 2.0 tools, students need to deal with these issues that are so important both in the classroom right now and in their professional lives in the future. See under 'Concerns'.

Web 2.0 is authentic

This book frequently uses authentic material from the internet. Whether it is a YouTube video of the BBC's latest news broadcast, an interview with a celebrity or politician on Vimeo or your favourite song from internet radio, Web 2.0 can provide constant and immediate access to authentic material relevant to the EFL lesson.

Web 2.0 is environmentally friendly

In times of global warming and excessive paper use regarding teaching materials, Web 2.0 offers you an environmentally friendly, sustainable and cheap alternative to paper. All the exercises and working procedures can be carried out in a virtual but graphically appealing and structured space. All the students' performances can be stored, commented on and marked and, only if really necessary, printed out.

Web 2.0 is motivational

Web 2.0 tools are popular with students. Social networking sites like Facebook, YouTube, FlickR etc meet the expectations of the teenage 'zeitgeist'. Web 2.0 brings what is relevant to teenagers into the classroom and connects to their interests, which is paramount to a successful teaching experience. In the EFL lesson, working with tools that the students are already acquainted with and interested in means they will be more highly motivated.

One reason why Web 2.0 tools are effective for teaching English is that there are plenty of tools for the Four Skills. For writing, there are hundreds of useful, didactically witty tools like PiratePad (Activity 3.1) that help students write various texts in a collaborative, creative and amicable atmosphere. Speaking and listening skills can also be intensively practised with tools such as Audioboo (Activity 4.2) and Spreaker (Activity 4.4), which encourage students to produce and listen to their spoken interactions by making a radio show or a podcast. Many Edu-Apps focus on the skill of reading.

Knowledge of the best apps makes a balanced, multi-methodological approach possible. Web 2.0 not only supports the four skills, but more than that, it integrates them. By using an application like Screenr (Activity 2.13), all four skills such as speaking, writing, listening and reading about a picture, can be integrated.

Web 2.0 is democratic

Educational applications let students experience a new learning culture. The teacher is no longer the sole, mono-directional provider of knowledge. Rather, they play the role of an equal participant within a community of practice (cf Wenger); everybody can learn from their peers within the context of Web 2.0 scenarios. By constantly communicating and collaborating with other group members, everyone will automatically get reflective input and feedback on their EFL performance. Many Web 2.0 apps support democratic learning settings where students form an intensive collaboration with their teacher or, even better, with a coach.

This more egalitarian learning environment usually generates a very positive attitude towards learning a language.

CONCERNS

Obviously there are various benefits for users/learners in the use of Web 2.0. However, there are certain concerns that should not be ignored:

Privacy and spam

In general, data and personal information is open and freely accessible with Web 2.0. Therefore, every user should be aware of the fact that *any information submitted to the internet cannot be taken back.* Users should always be cautious of the information they want to make public or submit to certain providers. Most services are offered by private companies. Sometimes by agreeing to the terms of service we, as users, relinquish private material which is then no longer considered to be our property.

Even though these applications have been tested, using them can (like registering on any website) mean the possibility of spam. In order to minimise its effects, as well as for sound practical didactic reasons, you should create a dedicated email account, as mentioned in 'Registration that makes sense' on page 13. **And ensure that your students do the same; this is something valuable that you can teach them about retaining privacy on the web.**

Plagiarism

The internet makes it extremely easy for almost anybody to find information about anything. It is tempting for people to help themselves to this information and pass it off as theirs. Students should, however, be encouraged to access and contrast different sources of information and then create their own materials through the cognitive processes involved, rather than just copying and pasting (without acknowledging, in many instances).

The transient nature of the web

Things come and go very quickly on the internet. Sometimes it is frustrating for people who may get the overwhelming feeling that they can never catch up with the speed at which things move, and with the sites and pages that come and go.

People sometimes store personal material, such as videos, pictures or documents using the online tools that are made available – but the very provider of the service, a private company, may disappear or may remove the site, thus leading to the loss of material. So, if you save any data – including text, images, music – on the web, it is worth saving it in at least two different places, and maybe using a hard drive for back up as well.

Quality

Since the internet has become so democratic, literally **any** person with internet access can provide material. So, many concerns about the quality and validity of, e.g., learning materials, are justified. However, this now enables you to help your students learn to scan and sift as to what is good quality and what is not. This is a very valuable life skill!

Copyright

Due to the fact that Web 2.0 is such a rich and varied media experience, the role of copyright is an important factor. Many images, videos, texts or music files should not be used for your social networking sites, blogs, websites etc. since they are copyright protected. However, many people do not abide by a fair use policy and still use these media. To be on the safe side, we strongly recommend that you look for material that is provided under the Creative Commons (CC) licence. In general, this is a copyright agreement relating to publicly available material that can be accessed and used by anyone, free of charge. Sites like FlickR offer many images with a CC licence.

AGE RESTRICTIONS ON WEBSITES

Many of the websites mentioned in this book have a restriction on children under 13 signing up/registering on the site and thus entering their personal details on it.

We strongly recommend that in your preparation you set aside the time necessary to check for yourself the terms and conditions of each site that you intend to use, to ensure that you will be able to comply with its restrictions as they apply to you and your students.

These restrictions are normally found in the terms and conditions and/ or the privacy policy. Some simply state that children under 13 may not register on the site. Others require parental consent. Yet others set up an arrangement that the teacher may register on behalf of the children, who may then access the site under the 'umbrella' provided by the teacher.

We have checked the conditions, and where we have found restrictions, we have given a brief indication of them in the teacher notes. However, it is possible that certain other restrictions may apply to you and/or your students, or that changes have been made since the time of writing, or that our checks missed a short but potentially relevant sentence lurking in the depths of these sometimes lengthy texts. We cannot accept any responsibility for you or your students not adhering to the terms and conditions of any website mentioned in this book and its associated web pages.

SOME BASIC INFORMATION ABOUT THE BOOK
Categories
The activities in this book have been classified into several categories: Teacher Tools, Visualisation, Collaboration, Audio and Writing. We also have an initial section devoted to apps especially for the teacher. However, whatever category the student activities fall into, they always encompass a range of skills, integrating these for a balanced and memorable learning experience. For example, the tools in the Audio category are not applications exclusively restricted to the skill of listening; writing skills can also be practised. In short, the division into categories is meant to be a very basic guide for you.

Didactics in, technology out
As stated earlier, the use of the Web 2.0 tools presented in this book does not require an advanced level of technical competency. Although some activities are more technically sophisticated than others, a strong emphasis has been placed on making the activities didactically useful and user-friendly, so that even if you are a novice user, or not tech-savvy, you can feel confident. If you are an advanced user, you will find that you can add more sophistication to provide an even greater impact.

Whatever your degree of mastery, you will find activities suitable for you. The main idea behind the book is to provide interactive, meaningful and highly motivational EFL activities in the context of Web 2.0 and the new learning technologies. Above all, what matters are the methodological underpinnings. Students and teachers can find new tools and new vehicles in Web 2.0, but methodology comes first.

Free websites and user-friendly applications
One main (and very welcome) principle behind Web 2.0 is that it is free of cost. All the tools presented are 100% free, and have been tested in many classrooms worldwide. Please be aware that for certain premium features of some applications presented, a fee will be charged. However, even though some sites have such premium features, the basic – and free – features are more than adequate for the activities proposed.

Registration that makes sense
Certain applications (but not all) require a simple registration process. We recommend that you create a second email account specifically for such registration processes (choosing a different password from your primary email). Furthermore, think of an internet ID/nickname (e.g. footballlover123) which is easily recognisable by your students and is the same for all the applications. You may or may not wish to have the same password for all these applications.

Web 2.0 and rapid developments
Due to the rapid developments of the internet and all its applications, and, because it is so easy to make changes to information on the internet, some of the procedures we have shown you will have been

updated and improved so that what you get on your screen may not be quite the same as what you see in the book. You may even find that some of the tools get removed eventually. So, we have suggested some alternative applications that are similar to the ones presented; even if some tools totally disappear, the book presents the activities in such a way that they can also be carried out with similar applications that are widely available.

Equipment
All of the activities require internet access. There are activities which can be done in the computer lab, some with just a single computer and a projector in the classroom, some with several laptops or netbooks or tablet PCs in the classroom, with smartphones, in the school library, with an interactive whiteboard or with a personal computer at home.

Language level
The activities cover a range of language levels, from beginner to advanced. At the back of the book is a quick reference guide, enabling you to check which activities will suit your class and circumstances best.

ICT skills
Having said that the focus will not be on technological expertise, every activity shows which ICT skills are required by teachers AND students. By doing a certain activity, students and teachers will improve the skills in question. Although some level of ICT competency is required, most applications and sites are fairly easy to use. Those students who are already familiar with a certain application or who quickly understand how to work with it, may actually become the teachers or experts; they can show you and their classmates how things are done. This is particularly interesting, because English then becomes the vehicle for real communication. By accessing sites and apps whose language is English, students are exposed to the language and work in it; more real communication!

Lead-in/follow-up steps/variations
In order to raise your students' interest and excitement, the activities have warm-up steps to make them curious about the tools they are about to use. The follow-up steps aim to round the activity off towards a successful outcome. Both the lead-in and follow-up steps are for the most part not technology-based.

In addition, the book offers variations to the main activity, suggesting different methodological approaches.

Useful resources
The Useful Resources section provides you with useful links that we hope you will find interesting concerning the use of new media in the classroom (links, tutorials, forums, etc.).

THE MIND THE APP WEBSITE includes:
- video tutorials exclusively produced for the apps from the book;
- the list of regularly updated app links from the book.

www.helblinglanguages.com/mindtheapp

CHAPTER 1
TEACHER TOOLS

1.1 Show you know!

Application:	Learning Apps, www.learningapps.org; lets you and your students create a great number of interactive quizzes.
Similar applications:	Classtools, www.classtools.net (see Activity 1.5); Kubbu, www.kubbu.com, ProProfs, www.proprofs.com/quiz-school (school edition); Quizlet, www.quizlet.com
Focus:	create various multi-media online exercises
Level (for the variation):	any
Age (for the variation):	13+ only
Time:	15–30 minutes
ICT skills:	browsing, typing
Equipment:	computer lab OR single computer

Do It Yourself

1 Go to www.learningapps.org; then click on 'English' in the top right corner.

2 If you have not signed up to this site, click on 'Login' (at top right), then click 'create a new account', complete the short online form, click on 'register account, and click on 'Create App' (at top).

3 Choose 'Multiple Choice Quiz', click on 'Create App' (see Image 1)

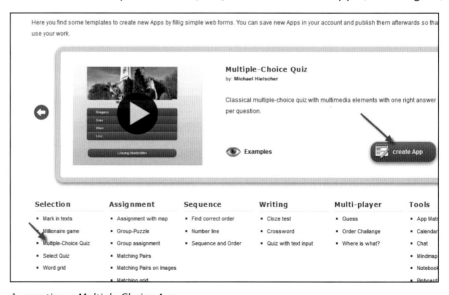

1: creating a Multiple Choice App

4   Fill in the fields. In our example, we will create a multiple choice quiz about London (see Image 2).

2: creating a multiple choice question

5   Type in the question (click on field 'text') and the right and wrong answers also giving feedback for each correct and wrong answer. (see Image 3). **Note:** you can alternatively add images, videos, etc. If you want to add another question to the quiz, click 'Add another element' (bottom).

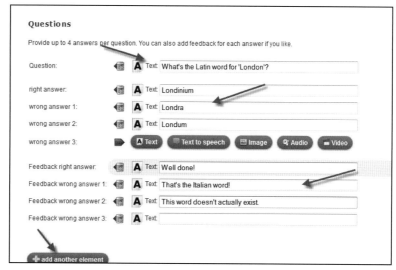

3: typing in the question and answers

6 After you have finished typing in your questions, scroll down and click 'Finish editing and preview App' (see Image 4)

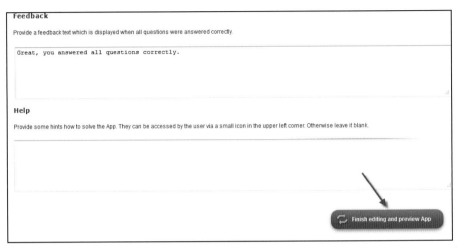

4: finish editing

7 Now you can preview the quiz. Then scroll down and click 'save app' (see Image 5).

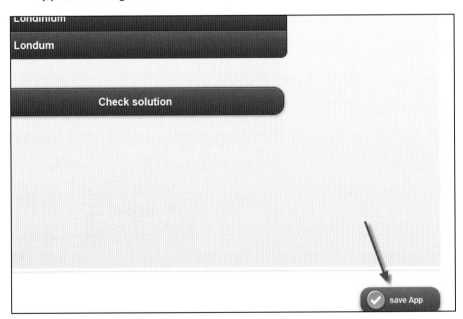

5: saving app

8 Your App is saved now. Scroll down and either copy the 'weblink' or the 'Fullscreen-link' for your students. **Note:** alternatively you can embed the exercise into a learning platform (see Image 6).

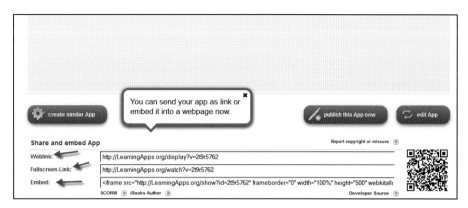

6: providing link for students

in class

Give your students the URL of your quiz ('Weblink' or 'Fullscreen-Link') and let them do it.

Variation – Students as quizmasters
Students can create quizzes for their classmates; this is a good way for them to recap certain EFL topics.

Learn more
There is a wide range of various exercise types. Learning Apps offers video tutorials for each exercise (see Image 7)

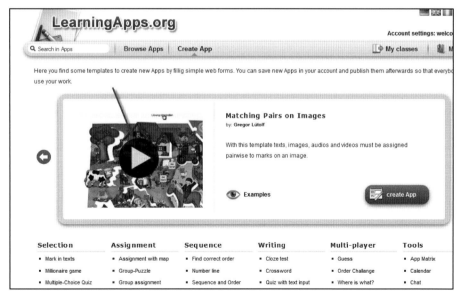

7: video tutorials

1.2 Share the good work

Application:	Authorstream, www.authorstream.com; lets you share and distribute Powerpoint presentations via the web. Authorstream is of great help if you do not want to send presentations with large files to your students via email (where you often get failure messages – files too big etc.). It is ideal for you if you often use Powerpoint presentations in your lessons and want to share your work.
Similar applications:	Slideshare, www.slideshare.net
Focus:	sharing Powerpoint presentations on the web
Level (for the variation):	all
Age (for the variation):	13+ only
Time:	10 minutes
ICT skills:	browsing, typing, copying & pasting, uploading
Equipment:	computer lab OR single computer

Do It Yourself

1   Register at www.authorstream.com (a basic account is free). If the window doesn't change when you have done this, click on the tiny Upload link at the very top right of the page.

2   Click 'Upload – upload from desktop' in the top control bar (see Image 1).

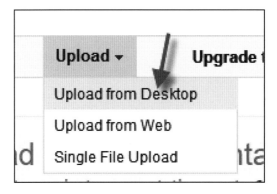

1: uploading a Powerpoint presentation

3   Then click 'Upload' again.

4   Choose the Powerpoint presentation you want to upload and show/distribute to your students, and click 'open'.

5   Then type in the required data.

> **Note:** If you want unregistered users to see your Powerpoint presentation, click 'public'. Then click 'Upload Now'.

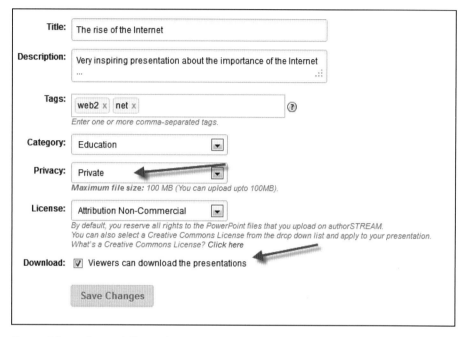

2: providing relevant information

6   Wait until the file has been uploaded and converted. This takes about 10 minutes, and you will get an email when your presentation is ready.

7   After your presentation has been uploaded successfully, click on 'My Stuff – My Presentation' in the top control bar.

8   Look for your presentation and copy the link.

in class

Give your link to your students so they can watch your Powerpoint presentation.

Variation – Presentation pool

Tell your students that they will be sharing their presentations via Authorstream. Use a backchannelling application like Todaysmeet (see Activity 3.4), where students can post a link to their uploaded presentation. Also, invite your students to add feedback/comments to their classmates' uploaded presentations; they can post a comment using the button directly below the relevant presentation.

1.3 Tube this – tube that ...

Application:	Quietube, www.quietube.com; removes all the lists, ads and other distracting features of YouTube.
Similar applications:	Tubechop, www.tubechop.com; Safeshare, www.safeshare.tv
Focus:	watch YouTube videos without any onscreen distractions
Level:	n/a
Age:	n/a
Time:	done in seconds
ICT skills:	browsing, typing, dragging & dropping
Equipment:	computer lab OR single computer; Mozilla Firefox is recommended as the browser of choice

Do It Yourself

1   Using the computer(s) you have in class, go to www.quietube. com. No registration required.

2   Drag the 'quietube' button into your browser's Bookmark (in the toolbar at top: see Image 1).

   Note: If you cannot see your bookmarks in the top browser field, click 'View – symbol bars/toolbars – bookmark symbol bar/ toolbar'.

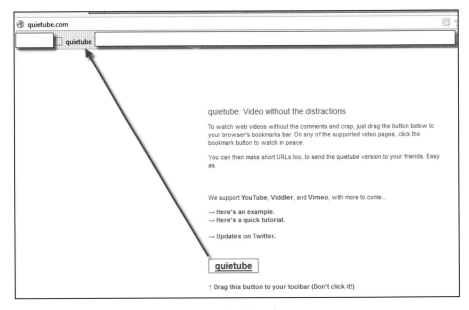

1: dragging the 'quietube' button into the bookmarks

1.3 Tube this – tube that …

3   Find a YouTube video you want to show in class and save its URL.

Open YouTube and type in the link to your video. When it appears, click the 'quietube' button in your bookmarks bar. Now you'll just see your video and nothing else – no ads and no trailers.

APPLICATION	LINK	DESCRIPTION
SchoolTube	www.schooltube.com	Video channel created and hosted by teachers and students. Mainly educational content.
TeacherTube	www.teachertube.com	Video channel for teachers by teachers. Educational content.
Next Vista	www.nextvista.org	A non-profit site run by a teacher. Highly educational content.
Snag Films	www.snagfilms.com	Good collection of documentaries.
Vimeo	http://vimeo.com	Similar to YouTube, better video quality.
DotSub	http://dotsub.com	Video collection with a wide range of subtitles in various languages.
CNN Student News	http://www.cnn.com/studentnews/	CNN news suitable for language learners.
Ted Talks	http://ted.com	Inspirational videos by experts on educational topics.
LangMedia Culture Talk	http://langmedia.fivecolleges.edu/culturetalk.html	Interviews with people from all over the world.
Clip Syndicate	www.clipsyndicate.com	News videos from all over the world.
22Frames	www.22frames.com	Videos for learners of English and the hard of hearing.
ESL basics	http://eslbasics.com	Videos for learners of English.
YouTube Teachers	http://www.youtube.com/teachers	YouTube Channel for teachers.

Credit to: Richard Byrne from http://www.freetech4teachers.com/

1.4 My YouTube Channel

Application: YouTube, www.youtube.com; a place to save all the YouTube videos you want to use in a lesson, presentation etc.

Focus: create YouTube playlists, retrieve videos easily

Level: n/a

Age: n/a

Time: done in minutes

ICT skills: browsing, typing, dragging & dropping

Equipment: computer with internet access

Do It Yourself

1 Go to www.youtube.com. Click 'Create Account' (see Image 1) and fill in the data.

1: create an account

If you see your name at the top of the page instead of 'Create Account', this tells you that your existing google or gmail account is linked to YouTube and you have been automatically signed in. So click on your name. In this case, be aware that *any personal information you have on that existing account is likely to show up in connection with any video you upload to YouTube.* If you don't want that to happen, the option of appearing on YouTube under a different identity should be given to you as you move forward on the site.

2 Click 'Video Manager' (see Image 2).

1.4 My YouTube Channel

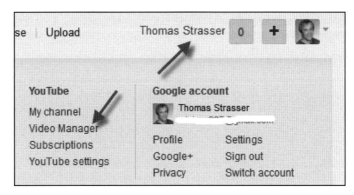

2: clicking Video Manager

3   Then click 'Playlist' and on the right-hand side see '+New playlist'. Click on that, and give your playlist a title (e.g. collection of news reports). Then click 'Create playlist' (see Image 3).

3: creating a playlist

5   You can choose whether your list is public or private (for your own use only) and several other settings below.

Then click 'Save' (at top right of the page).

6   Now your playlist is ready for you to add the videos you want.

Here is how to add a video:

- Search for a video for your EFL lesson (e.g. BBC news Obama) on YouTube.
- Click on the video and watch it before showing it in class.
- Then click 'Add to' (below the picture). Sign in again if necessary, and when the Playlist menu opens below, click on your newly created list to add the YouTube video. Click on 'Close'. You may find you have to wait until the video has finished playing for the title to be added to the playlist.

7   To delete a video from a playlist, click on its name on your Videos page, then on the top right of the list page, click on 'Edit'. Tick the video(s) you want to delete, click on the dropdown arrow beside Actions (at the top of the list) and pick 'Remove videos from playlist'.

8   You can also upload videos of your own to YouTube by following the Upload procedure. If you don't want these to contain advertisements, first go back to the screen shown in Step 2 and click on YouTube Settings; in the Overview that appears, you will see the option 'Do not allow advertisements to be displayed beside my videos'. Click on 'Save'.

in class

When you want to show a video, you do not have to search for it on YouTube or remember the link of the video; instead you open your YouTube Channel by going to www.youtube.com/<nameofyouraccount>, or by going to YouTube Channel and logging in, then picking the videos you want to show.

Top Tip 1: When you have a number of videos for your EFL lesson, the YouTube Channel helps keep things in order for you. For example, you can create a list for each of your classes or theme-based lists: money, free time, friends, music etc. Your students can then easily access any category.

Top Tip 2: When surfing the net in preparation for your lesson, you may come across a video that you feel would be useful for your class – however, 10 minutes later, you may have forgotten the link or the name of the video. If, however, you have set up a YouTube Channel, you can save the video in a safe (and easily remembered) place with just a couple of clicks!

1.5 Tool time …

Application:	Classtools, www.classtools.net; lets you and your students create educational content and games. Classtools is an ideal tool to begin or conclude a lesson.
Similar applications:	Quizlet, www.quizlet.com; Proprofs, www.proprofs.com (see Activity 1.1), Kubbu, www.kubbu.com
Focus:	create educational games, activities
Level (for the variations):	elementary–advanced
Age (for the variations):	any – no registration required
Time:	10–60 minutes
ICT skills:	browsing, typing, copying & embedding, dragging & dropping
Equipment:	computer lab OR single computer

Do It Yourself

1   Go to www.classtools.net. You do not need to register or log in to use this site. This activity uses only a few of the many Classtools activities; when you have time, you might like to check out all the subjects and activity templates in the yellow box in the top right corner on the www.classtools.net home page.

2   But for now, try out the Game Generator. From the 'Select a Template' dropdown menu, click on 'Game Generator', then 'Arcade Game Generator'.

3   Type in a title for your quiz (in our example, it's 'past tense forms'). Then type in your questions and answers (i.e. base form and past form), using the following format: question*answer (see Image 1). **Note:** You must type in a minimum of ten questions.

    Top Tip 1: You can prepare your Q&As in a word processing program and then copy and paste them into Classtools.

    Top Tip 2: If you are generating your Q&As in Classtools, it is a good idea to copy them into a text document on your computer.

    Click on 'Free choice [Default]' and choose a game type (see below), then press 'OK'. Don't forget to provide a password so that you can edit your questions (see Image 1). Then press 'OK' again.

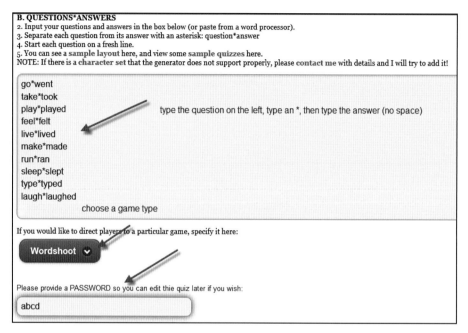

B. QUESTIONS*ANSWERS

2. Input your questions and answers in the box below (or paste from a word processor).

3. Separate each question from its answer with an asterisk: question*answer

4. Start each question on a fresh line.

5. You can see a **sample layout** here, and view some **sample quizzes** here.

NOTE: If there is a **character set** that the generator does not support properly, please **contact me** with details and I will try to add it!

```
go*went
take*took
play*played          type the question on the left, type an *, then type the answer (no space)
feel*felt
live*lived
make*made
run*ran
sleep*slept
type*typed
laugh*laughed
              choose a game type
```

If you would like to direct players to a particular game, specify it here:

Wordshoot ⌄

Please provide a PASSWORD so you can edit thie quiz later if you wish:

abcd

1: basic settings

4   Now your game is ready. Try the game out yourself before giving it to your students. When you have finished, click on 'Give Up' or click on the 'back' button of your browser.

5   If you want to add questions or edit your quiz (e.g. change the game type), click 'Edit this quiz' in the bottom left corner. You will need your password (type it in and click 'Submit').

6   To provide this quiz to your students, click on click on 'Share this Quiz', then 'URL link/Embed code' (see Image 2). Then copy the URL of the quiz and save it.

   Top Tip: This URL allows you to edit your questions, using your password, any time you like.

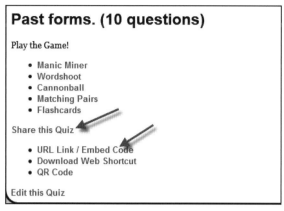

2: providing the quiz to students

in class

Tell your students that you are going to play educational games. Give them the link you copied earlier. Give them plenty of time to play a range of games from the site.

Variation 1 – Vocab guru
Use Classtools games (Flashcards, Memory etc.) for any vocabulary-learning sequences (animals, food etc.) you have created for your class.

Variation 2 – The missing link
You can use Classtools for text-coherence exercises. Students should match sentence halves about text that they have read, or useful phrases (such as expressing their point of view) etc.

Variation 3 – Competitive history
Use the Arcade Game Generator (Flashcards, Memory, Wordshooter etc.) for teaching historical/cultural aspects in your EFL lessons.
Let students match e.g. memorable historical events with certain personalities, people etc, e.g.: *Civil disobedience in India → Mahatma Gandhi*, or *March on Washington 60s → Martin Luther King*.
Or: Classtools is good for cross-curricular topics. Students create their own games in English from what they have learnt in other subjects.

Top Tip: be careful students choose appropriate topic fields when using 'Wordshooter'. It is not acceptable to shoot cities or people so they should avoid these topic areas.

1.6 Hey, teacher, tell me what to do!

Application:	mailVU, www.mailVU.com; lets you and your students create short video messages without having to register.
Similar applications:	Eyejot, http://corp.eyejot.com/
Focus:	create video emails or video messages
Level (for the variations):	all levels
Age (for the variations):	any
Time:	5+ minutes, depending on length of exercises
ICT skills:	browsing, typing, copying and pasting
Equipment:	computer with internet access that will allow access by Adobe Flash Player; webcam, microphone (stand-alone, in headset or built into laptop) and speakers

Do It Yourself

1 Go to www.mailVU.com, in general, there is no need to register.

2 You are going use mailVU to send your students a video message describing a task you will set them for homework, e.g. texts they have to read or exercises they have to do.

3 Make sure your webcam is on and your microphone is working.

4 Then click 'Record Video', then 'Allow' (Adobe Flash Player) and give your instructions, present your tasks etc, click the Record button (see Image 1). When you are finished, click the 'Stop' button.

1: record button

5 After recording, click 'Send' (if you want to email your message to your students) or 'Share' (to get a URL for your students to see the video) (see Image 2).

2: 'Send' or 'Share'

6 If you click 'Send', you will just need to complete the popup box; if you click 'Share', copy/note the URL (see Image 3) and give it to your students.

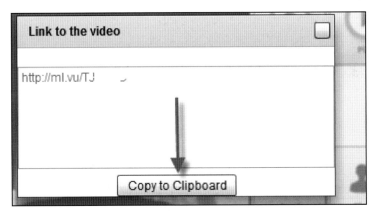

3: copying the URL

in class

At the end of a lesson, give your students the URL with your video message. Tell them to open the link at home.

follow-up

1 At home, students open the link and follow the video homework instructions. The big advantage of mailVU is that students can listen over and over again to instructions for an assignment.

Note: For students who do not have a computer at home, take them aside and tell them the homework verbally.

Variation 1 – Video quiz

You can also create a short quiz show for your students. Record several EFL-related questions (e.g. cultural studies, vocab, grammar forms etc.). Students watch the video and hand in the answers next lesson. Or, you can discuss the answers as a class.

Variation 2 – Tricky text

On mailVU, read a text that is known to the students (either you have already read the text together in class or students have read it as an assignment). But, this time, include several mistakes (pronunciation, content mistakes, grammar mistakes, vocab mistakes etc.) in your reading. Students try to identify the mistakes.

Variation 3 – Summary – the visual way

Your students can use mailVU too. Tell them that they can use it in order to summarise a novel, newspaper article, poem etc. they have read in an EFL lesson. Students then give you the URL of the video they have made.

Variation 4 – Practice makes perfect

In order for your students to practise intonation, stress patterns and certain sounds, tell them to read a text you have handed out to them. They can practise saying the text aloud, and when they feel confident enough, they record themselves with mailVU to get instant feedback – very valuable!

Variation 5 – Presentations

Students work around a topic (ideally something that they have just seen in class) and record a short video.

Variation 6 - Verbal feedback

You can use mailVU to give spoken/videotaped feedback to your students (e.g. after an assignment, written text, presentation, etc.)

CHAPTER 2
VISUALISATION

2.1

'I have a dream'

Application:	Wordle, www.wordle.net; generates 'word clouds' from text that you provide. The clouds give greater prominence to words that appear more frequently in the source text.
Similar applications:	Tagxedo, www.tagxedo.com; Tagul, www.tagul.com
Focus:	interpreting and creating visual input
Level:	intermediate–advanced
Age:	any – no registration required
Time:	30–40 minutes
ICT skills:	copying, pasting, browsing for texts
Equipment:	a computer with internet access and a projector

Do It Yourself

1 Depending on which version of the lead-in activity you use, prepare either one or two sets of slips of paper for each group of students:
   • for Lead-in 1: a set with a memorable statement on each slip, from Martin Luther King's 'I have a dream' speech (e.g. 'But we refuse to believe that the bank of justice is bankrupt').
   • for Lead-in 2: a set with famous quotes by famous people (e.g. John F. Kennedy: 'Ich bin ein Berliner', Barack Obama: 'Yes, we can'), plus a set with pictures of the people whose words you have quoted.

2 Find some digital texts (texts on your computer, internet etc.) relevant to the topic you want to teach and save them. Copy the first text (select the whole text (Ctrl-A), then either right-click on it and pick 'Copy', or hit Ctrl-C).

3 Go to www.wordle.net and at the top of the page click 'Create' (see Image 1).

Note: If you find Wordle doesn't work at first, you will probably need to reconfigure your firewall or web content filter, or enable Java applets to run in your browser.

Note: Even if Wordle works straight away, we suggest checking which version of Java your computer is running. The distributors, Sun Microsystems, strongly advise that if your computer has a version older than Version 7 Update 5, you completely remove the earlier version asap and replace it with 7:5. (Java is used not just for Wordle, but also for several other applications on your computer.)

2.1 'I have a dream'

1: the Create button

4   Click in the box near the top and paste in (Ctrl-V) the copied text; here, it was the 'I have a dream' speech by Martin Luther King (find this online by searching on "I have a dream", using the double quote marks to make the search engine find exactly those words). Click 'Go' (see Image 2). *Do not hit the return key* – that will just create a new line at the end of the text.

2: clicking 'Go'

5   Your word cloud displaying the words of Martin Luther King's speech should be visible now (see Image 3).

3: a completed word cloud

6   Now create some more Wordles from the texts you have saved, and save them for the lesson.

2.1 'I have a dream'

Lead-in

1 Tell your students to form groups of about 4, depending on the size of the class.

2 Hand out the sets of Martin Luther King slips, one set to each group. Do not tell your students that the quotes are from MLK's speech.

3 Tell your students to discuss the meaning of the statements in groups. Students can also focus on aspects such as metaphors, symbols, etc.

4 Discuss the students' findings as a class. Some students will definitely recognise the text.

Alternative lead-in

1 Tell your students to form groups of 4.

2 Hand out the slips with quotes by famous people to each group. Also hand out the set of pictures of these people.

3 Tell your students to match the quotes with the pictures.

4 Discuss the answers as a class. Talk about these people and give input on their achievements.

Online

1 Open Wordle and show your students a wordle created from one of your texts.

2 Set up groups in your class; explain that this type of display is called a 'tag cloud' and they will have 10 minutes to analyse it. Let them guess where this text might be taken from, what kind of text it is, and what it is about.

3 Then let the groups interpret the tag cloud as a class. If they have problems interpreting the cloud, give them a hint about the varying sizes of the words. Ask the students: *How come the word 'xxx' is so big in this context?* Try to collect as many interpretations by the students as possible.

Variation 1 – Using songs
Especially suitable for lower-level groups, but good also for higher-level ones, are song lyrics. Activities include:

- **Lexical work:** many students love to learn new words in a graphically appealing context. By working with tag clouds, students recognise the relevance/importance of certain words in a certain context.
- **Interpretation:** tag clouds may help students interpret the song's message.
- **Cultural studies:** the appearance of certain culturally specific words means that you can teach your students about the special features of a certain country/city, nation or culture.
- **Stylistics:** by displaying song lyrics in a compact visual way, tag clouds help the student make judgements about the qualitative aspects of a certain song (i.e. repetition, use of simple register, rhymes etc.).

4: tag cloud of the song 'Old MacDonald'

Variation 2 – Using biographies

With learners of all levels, you can use biographies (taken from, e.g., Wikipedia) to work with tag clouds. Before the class starts, create a word cloud with Wordle using your chosen biography. Then delete* certain words explicitly associated with the person, such as the name. In class, let the students guess the famous person in the tag cloud.

* To delete a word from the tag cloud, right-click on the word and press 'Remove "xxx"'.

5: Shakespeare biography in Wordle

Variation 3 – Mindmapping

You can also use tag clouds for mindmapping sequences when beginning a new topic:

1   Be sure that the projector is switched off.
2   Students form groups of 3–5.
3   Tell the students that they will have 10 minutes to collect words/ phrases they associate with a certain topic (here, the USA), and work out their 'Top 3' words (i.e. the words they associate the most strongly with the topic).
4   Then one representative of each group types their Top 3 words into Wordle.
5   When all the words have been typed in, create a word cloud and project it onto the wall.
6   Then start a discussion on why certain words appear the biggest.

6: mindmapping carried out by students (topic: USA)

Variation 4 – Repetition check

Students can also use Wordle in order to check whether or not they have repeated words a lot. When they see that certain words appear very big (e.g. linkers like 'and', 'however' etc.), they know that they may need to find synonyms or other ways of wording their text.

More Wordle functions

- You can print your tag cloud and copy it onto an OHP.
- You can change settings like colour, font etc. (see Image 7).
- You can change the design of your tag cloud (see Image 7).

7: more functions

follow-up

1 For homework, tell your students to pick a historical figure they associate with or who they might find appealing/interesting.

2 Using Wordle, they should create a tag cloud at home, ready to print it out in class, or show it on a projector.

3 In class, students should show their tag cloud and use it as an aid to talk about this personality.

More ideas

http://www.wordle.net/advanced

2.2 'Let's do the time warp again'

Application:	Capzles, www.capzles.com; allows students to create highly visual chronological timelines. For each event, students can add comments, photos, documents etc.
Similar applications:	Tripline, www.tripline.net (see Activity 2.9); Scribblemaps, www.scribblemaps.com
Focus:	create timelines of events/chronological photo stories
Level:	pre-intermediate–advanced
Age:	13+ only
Time:	60 minutes
ICT skills:	uploading, browsing
Equipment:	computer lab OR single computer, pen drive/flash drive/USB stick for each student, projector
Preparation:	Before this lesson, your students – either at home or in the lab in a run-up lesson – will need to find some photos from a field trip, language trip etc. and save them on a pen drive/USB stick/flash drive. Tell them to check that all the photos are the right way up.

Do It Yourself

1 Go to www.capzles.com and join.

2 Click on 'Create' > 'New Capzle' (see Image 1).

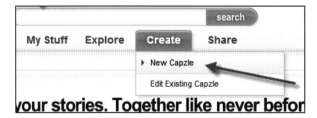

1: creating a new Capzle

3 Now you can upload some pictures. In our example, photos from a trip to New York will be uploaded. Click on 'Add content', then 'Upload directly onto my timeline' and then 'add files' (see Image 2).

2: uploading pictures

4   Then choose the pictures to be uploaded; to upload more than one, Ctrl-click on each of them (see Image 3).
Top Tip: You can also upload videos, mp3s, pdfs, Powerpoint files, etc. Be careful with copyright issues!

3: marking several pictures for uploading

5   Once the photos have uploaded, the next step is to put them into chronological order. Click on a photo, adjust the date/time and add a comment (see Images 4 and 5).

2.2 'Let's do the time warp again'

4: *adjusting uploaded pictures*

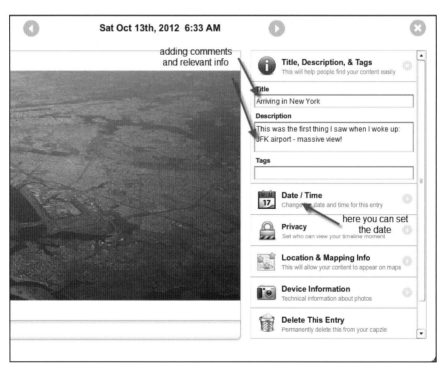

5: *adding date and comments*

CHAPTER 2: VISUALISATION

6   When you have entered the details you want, click on the grey circle with a right-pointing arrow inside it above the photo, to move on to the next one. Repeat these steps with each photo you have uploaded. In the end, you will have created a chronological, highly visual photo timeline.

7   To finalise the story, add a title (click 'Add a title and description'). Then click on 'I'm finished'.

in class

Lead-in
1   Ask your students to show their pictures to the class, using the projector.

2   Tell them that they can talk freely about their pictures.

Online
1   Tell your students to go to www.capzles.com and help them join. Depending on the level of your students, you can explain everything in English so they become acquainted with IT-specific vocabulary (*log on*, *register*, *browser* etc.).

2   Students click on 'Create > New Capzle' (see Image 1).

3   Now the students can upload their pictures; tell them about Ctrl-clicking to upload more than one.

4   Next the students put their photos into chronological order and add a comment. Tell them to write in a clear, understandable and informative way when adding the comment.

5   They repeat these steps with each photo they have uploaded, then add a title and description to create their photo timeline.

6   Then they can share the link to their photo story with their classmates or you (click 'Share' in the top left corner) to give the opportunity for feedback.

Variation 1 – A day in the life of ...
You can ask higher-level students to create an interactive timeline of a famous historical person, celebrity or historical event. Tell the students they should do some research about this person, finding milestones in their lives and briefly commenting on them.

Variation 2 – Learning journal

In order to record the learning process, you can also show students how to create a learning journal with Capzles. When studying for a test, students can define their learning process by uploading a picture, pdf or text file associated with the topic to be learnt. By using the comment function, students can record their progress (e.g. 'I know a lot about Immigration in Britain' or 'I need to focus on tenses').

Variation 3 – Video collage

With students of all levels, you can also use Capzles for uploading videos. e.g. for an essay-writing competition. Students should write a text about a certain topic (e.g. *the best moment in my life*) and video themselves saying the text aloud on their mobiles. Each sends his/her video to one student who uploads them onto Capzles. The student shares the link with all his/her classmates so that they can add comments or give feedback. The result is you have a timeline of spoken essays.

follow-up

1 Based on their Capzles of a field trip or something similar, ask your students to write an adventure essay or an account of this trip.

More ideas

http://www.capzles.com/#/explore-capzles/?filter=popular

2.3 Vocab visualiser

Application: PhasR, http://www.pimpampum.net/phrasr/; makes written sentences visible as pictures.

Focus: visualise written sentences

Level: elementary–advanced

Age: any – no registration is required

Time: 30 minutes

ICT skills: browsing, typing

Equipment: computer lab OR single computer, plus either an OHT projector, an OHT transparency reel or several sheets, non-permanent OHT pens and, optional, a handout (see below) – or an interactive whiteboard

Preparation: Prepare a vocabulary list with the words you want your students to learn. Just type the English words to be learnt – nothing else – on a handout or the OHT.

Do It Yourself

1   Go to www.pimpampum.net/phrasr/.

2   Type a word in a meaningful contextualised sentence into the box on the screen. In our example (see Image 1) the word 'collects' has been put into a sentence. Then click 'Start!'

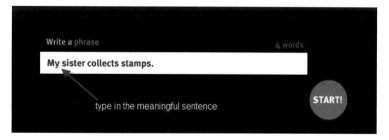

1: typing in a meaningful sentence

3   The sentence appears in visual form, making it easier for students to learn the new word. Students can learn even more effectively by choosing pictures they associate best with the word (see Images 2 and 3).

2: adapting images to your own ideas

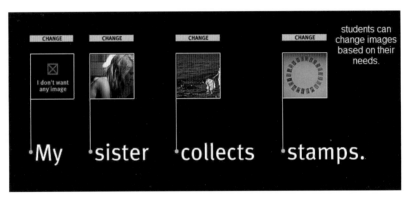

3: a sentence!

4   Add in a title and your name, and click 'Publish!' to see the sentence in larger pictures.

in class

Lead-in

1   Ask your students to think up a simple (subject + verb + object) sentence in English, for example: *The monster eats chocolate.* Tell your students to keep their sentence secret and to draw a sketch of it on a piece of paper.

2   Tell your students that you are going to play a guessing game. Pick a confident and artistic student to draw his/her sketch from the sheet of paper onto an OHT transparency while the projector is switched on so students can guess the picture while he/she is drawing it. The student who guesses the sentence first draws the next picture. Play this game two or three times.

Online
1   In the computer lab, hand out or display your vocabulary list. Tell your students that they should use an online dictionary to translate the English words into their mother tongue. When they have done this, they should go to www.pimpampum.net/phrasr/.

2   They should then think of a meaningful sentence for the first new word, and type this into PhasR. Now the sentence appears in visual form, and they can choose the pictures they associate best with the word.

3   They can then add in a title and their name and click 'Publish!' to see the sentence in larger pictures.

Variation 1 – Mini photo story
Your students can use PhasR to create mini stories in photos.

Variation 2 – Show my pics
If there is a projector or an interactive whiteboard in class, encourage your students to display what they have done. Some of them will come up with highly creative ideas!

2.4 Glogster it!

Note:	the screenshots are taken from the premium teacher account. While writing this book, Glogster had slightly different layouts for the regular and teacher accounts.
Application:	Glogster, http://edu.glogster.com (free premium teacher accounts available!); lets you create an interactive desktop. Students can practise various EFL topics by browsing through given websites, watching YouTube videos, doing various internet-based exercises, reading relevant articles etc. Students can also create their own glogs for presentations, collages etc.
Focus:	creating interactive desktops/working space for students
Level:	intermediate–advanced
Age:	under 13s may register on the site only with permission from parent/guardian
Time:	depends on content
ICT skills:	browsing, typing, copying & pasting, uploading
Equipment:	computer lab OR single computer.

Do It Yourself

1   Register at edu.glogster.com. Registration is required in order to save 'glogs' and to allow your students to use the site. At the end of the registration process your 'Dashboard' will appear and, in the panel stating the basis on which you have registered (probably 'Single Free Teacher'), will be your Teacher Code. You need to make a note of this to enable your students to register.

2   Click on 'Create New Glog'.

3   Start by picking a template. Do this by clicking 'Classic Glog' (right hand side).

4   Remove the announcement; to do this, click on it once, and then click on the Trashcan in the Edit bar (see Image 1).

2.4 Glogster it!

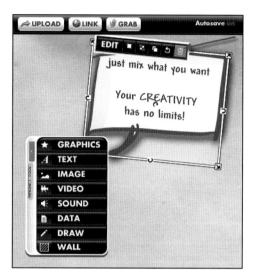

1: deleting remaining objects

5   Now you are ready to start. In our example, we are going to design an interactive desktop for students; through Glogster you will be able to give them videos, handouts, links, exercises etc on the topic 'Australia'.

6   The first step is to create an appealing headline for the topic. Click on 'text' and choose a design that suits you best (see Image 2). After you have decided on an appropriate template, click 'use it'. Then close the window by clicking on the 'x' in the right top corner.

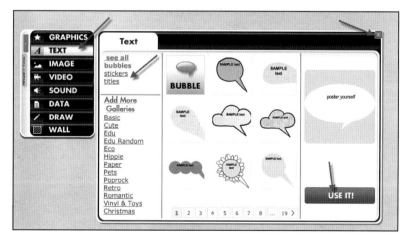

2: choosing the design for the headline

7   Then adjust your text sign by clicking and dragging it wherever you want to.

8   Now click 'edit', delete 'poster yourself' (see Image 3), and write your text into the text field. In our example it's going to be 'Australia'. Then click 'Okay'.

3: typing text into text field

9   Click on the text field again. Then click 'edit' and you will have a wide range of settings (font, effects etc. – see Image 4).

4: settings

10 You can also add images and videos to your interactive desktop. Click 'Image' or 'Video' in the left-hand control bar.

11 You can upload images either from your computer (click on 'upload') or from the internet (click on 'link').To get an image from the internet, open Google Image Search or FlickR etc., choose an image that is not subject to copyright restrictions, (see Top Tip 2 on next page) and right-click on it. Click 'copy image URL' or, if you don't have that option, 'copy image location' or similar. Then go

back to Glogster and paste the link into the field 'Add image from the web' (see Image 6). Then click 'add to your files'.

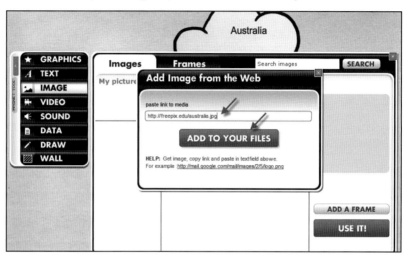

5: pasting an image URL

Top Tip 1: For image search, the author recommends the free, open source browser Mozilla Firefox due to its user-friendly menu and excellent security.

Top Tip 2: In order to use royalty-free images in Google, click 'Images', then 'extended search' (next to the field where you type in your search query) and then click 'images available for re-use'.

12 Now your image is stored in your Glogster folder. Click on it once, then on 'Use it' (see Image 6). Then click 'Close' by clicking the 'x' in the top right corner.

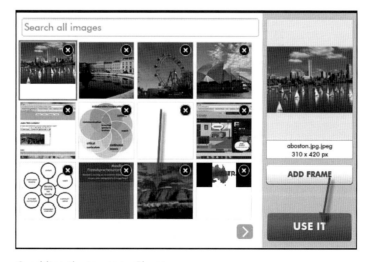

6: adding the image to Glogster

13 Adjust the image by clicking on it once and using the arrows in the corners of the image (minimise/maximise). (see Image 7).

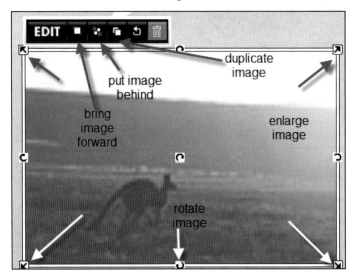

7: adjusting the image

14 You can also add a YouTube video to Glogster. Open www. youtube.com and find a relevant video. Copy the URL from the video. Go back to Glogster and, in the control bar on the left, click 'Video'. Click on 'link' and paste the URL. Then click 'Add to your files'.

15 As in Step 12, click on your video and click 'Use it'.

   Note: The video can only be played when you have finished your glog.

16 You can also upload audio files by clicking 'Sound' in the control bar. Then follow Steps 11 and 12.

17 One outstanding feature of Glogster is that you can add links to grammar exercises, handouts, useful websites etc to your fields. Click on an image or text you would like to add a link to; in our example, this will be a Wikipedia article about the Sydney Opera House. So open Wikipedia to find a suitable article and copy its URL.

18 Now click 'edit'. Then click on the little chain symbol, paste the URL from the Wikipedia article and click 'Apply' (see Image 8). Then click 'OK'.

8: pasting the URL from the YouTube video

19 You can also add grammar exercises from informative websites plus your own handouts and links to various text fields, images and videos. Create a new text field (see Steps 6-9) and add the URL of your materials. You can add as many videos, images and links as you wish.

20 To change the background (the wall) of your glog, click on 'Wall' in the control bar as you did at the start.

21 Finally, click 'Save and Publish' at the top, then enter the name of your glog, click the category and choose 'Finished', then click 'Save' (see Image 9).

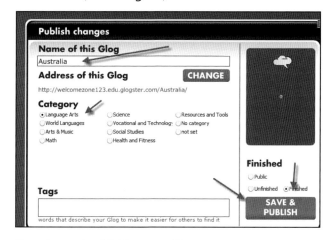

9: saving and publishing your Glog

2.4 Glogster it!

22 Copy the URL of your glog and keep it for the lesson.

in class

Lead-in
1 Tell your students that today they will be doing various tasks on an interactive desktop called Glogster.

Online
1 Give your glog link to the students. Tell them that they should click all the links, images, videos in order to explore the topic Australia. They are free to choose which activity they would like to start with.

2 Walk around the computer lab and give feedback.

3 After students have finished, compare their individual tasks within the class.

follow-up

Next time, if there is an interactive whiteboard or a projector in the classroom, let your students present their glogs to the class.

Variation 1 – This is me ...
Let students design a short profile of themselves, including little texts (hobbies etc.) videos, images and favourite links.
Make sure younger learners know how to use Glogster first.

Variation 2 – Topical glog
With students at higher levels, you can use Glogster at a topical level. Think of a controversial topic (e.g. the financial crisis) and let students work on this topic using Glogster. They can easily include relevant articles, interviews, images etc. Have your students present their glogs.

Variation 3 – Book glog
With students at higher levels, you can also invite them to present book reports with Glogster. By including various links (author's website, websites with reviews, videos about author/book etc.) and writing little texts (with the text field), a book report becomes more dynamic and interactive.

Variation 4 – Celebrity glog
A glog about a favourite celebrity can be quite motivating especially for young learners. A big advantage of a glog about a celebrity is that there is plenty of material (videos, interviews, audio etc.) on the web. Also, students can write little texts about their celebrities (why they like them so much).

2.4 Glogster it!

Variation 5 – Quotations glog

For learners at higher levels, have them collect famous statements/ quotes on a certain topic (e.g. internet, Facebook etc.). Students should post the statements (audio, video, text) and interpret them using all the various media available on glogster.

Learn more

http://www.glogster.com/explore/Education

2.5 Photostory 2.0

Application: Photovisi, www.photovisi.com; lets your students create graphically appealing photo stories.

Similar application: Animoto, www.animoto.com (cf. Activity 2.12)

Focus: creating photo stories

Level: intermediate–advanced

Age: 13+

TIme: 60 minutes

ICT skills: browsing, typing, copying & pasting, uploading

Equipment: computer lab OR single computer, USB stick/pen drive

Preparation: Using a text type or topic you are discussing at the moment, tell your students to bring a pen drive/flash drive/USB stick with some images (e.g. pictures of themselves, pictures of a beach, market square etc.) that they could use to illustrate a story about their summer holidays.

Do It Yourself

1 Go to www.photovisi.com and click on 'Register'.

2 Go through the signup procedure. Then click 'Start creating'.

3 Click on a template (background) for your photo story (see Image 1). You can change the background later, if you like.

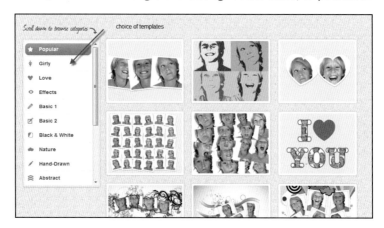

1: choosing a template for your photo story

4 Then click 'add items' and choose images from your computer or webcam. Our example shows how to start uploading photos from a computer (see Image 2).

2.5 Photostory 2.0

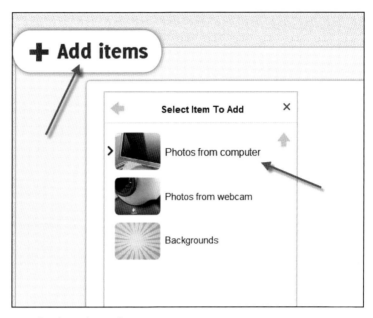

2: uploading photos from computer

5   After you have uploaded the images you want, you can adjust the place and size of the images. Click on an image and drag the dots to maximise/minimise the pictures (see Image 3).

3: adjusting size of images

6   Click 'add text' (right hand side) to add a description to each image; type into the text box under 'Text Tool' and click 'Add text to collage'. You can adjust the text size as well, again using the dots around the text (see Image 4).

4: adjusting the size/font of the text

7   After you have finished your photo story, click 'Finish'. Choose your download resolution and then 'continue' below.

8   Now you can download your photo story (as a jpeg (.jpg) file).

9   Finally, you have the option of sharing it on Facebook or Twitter, or emailing it. Click on 'download collage' and/or email it to yourself, ready for your lesson. You can also close the 'Share your collage' window, and click on 'Download collage'.

in class

Lead-in

1 Tell your students that they are going to create a digital photo story and that you are going to show one you created yourself to give them an idea of what they are about to do.

Online

1   Open your email with your photo story and click the link to display it to your students (or, if you prefer, forward the email with the photostory to each of them). Tell them that they are going to produce a similar one, about their summer holiday.

2   Tell them to register at www.photovisi.com.

3   Explain to them how Photovisi works.

4   Give your students plenty of time to create their photo story. They can use either their own images or ones they find on the internet during the writing process.

5   After your students have finished, tell them to save their photo story on their USB sticks and bring them along for the next lesson.

Variation – Visual book report
Students at higher levels can make a photo story of a book they have had to read in the course of their studies.

follow-up

1   In the next lesson, let your students present their photo story to the class.

2   So your students can practise text-specific writing skills, have them write a sequel to their picture story.

2.6 Tune my handout!

Application: Signgenerator, www.signgenerator.org; lets you choose from a wide range of well-known templates. By adding the text suitable for your classroom needs into a field, Signgenerator converts the templates to show your text.

Focus: embedding appealing graphics into handouts, blogs, presentations etc.

Level: all levels

Age: any – no registration required

Time: variable, depending on handout, website, presentation etc.

ICT skills: browsing, typing, copying & pasting

Equipment: computer lab OR single computer

Do It Yourself

1   Go to www.signgenerator.org. At the time of writing, no registration is required. (NB 'Look here!' at top right leads to an ad, not part of the program.)

2   Scroll down to look through the vast number of themes. (NB The author is *not* responsible for the content of Signgenerator!)

    Top Tip 1: In order to find a particular theme more easily, press Ctrl+F and type in your query. E.g. if you want to create a handout with images about crime, type 'crime'.

    Top Tip 2: However, it is also worth spending a bit of time looking through the various templates (i.e. photo backgrounds) one by one.

3   After you have found an interesting link, click on it. Then wait for the template to open. In our example, we have clicked on 'Posting a Fence Sign'.

4   Type in the text you want into the 'Your Text' box, adjust the settings (font etc.) and click 'Change the message' (see Image 1).

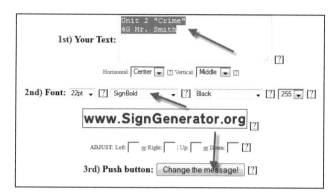

1: typing in the text for the template

5   Now your template for your handout, interactive whiteboard etc. is done! (See Image 2.) Right-click on the picture and click 'Save image as …'. Now you can use the template for handouts etc. If you want to save more than one image, you will need to generate a different name for each one – a new name doesn't come up automatically.

2: finished template

Lead-in

1   Ask your students about the typical features of a newspaper headline. With students at higher levels you can focus on linguistic or stylistic aspects (use of *to* + infinitive, frequent use of present simple, word plays, etc.) or on genre-specific observations (headline depends on the newspaper type/quality, so serious headlines vs. catchy ones etc.) Collect the students' ideas on the board.

2.6 Tune my handout!

Online

1   Using the search query (Ctrl + F) for 'newspaper', you can let your students use the templates in order to write short newspaper intros. E.g. click the 'Newspaper Clip Generator' link and let students write headlines and introduction using an authentic newspaper template (see Image 3).

3: writing newspaper clips

follow-up

1   For homework, students should find a newspaper article/headline looking at the aspects discussed in Lead-in Step 1. Let them briefly present their newspaper headlines in class and discuss them.

2.7 Arty stories

Application:	Storybird, www.storybird.com; lets your students create highly visual picture stories with given templates by young artists.
Similar application:	Zooburst, www.zooburst.com (see Activity 5.4)
Focus:	creating picture stories with pieces of art
Level:	beginner–intermediate.
Age:	any; under 18s are asked to review the T&C with parent or guardian, and the parents of under 13s will be emailed to gain their approval for their children to use the site
Time:	60 minutes
ICT skills:	browsing, typing, copying & pasting
Equipment:	computer lab OR single computer

Do It Yourself

1   Register with a teacher account at www.storybird.com. You need to register in order to save your stories.

2   Write your own story.

3   Click on 'Create' in the top control bar.

4   Then choose the template of a piece of art you like to write your story with (see Image 1). Then click 'Start a Storybird'.

1: choosing an art template

5   Now you can start with your first drawing. Choose a template you like or you find appropriate for your story. Click on it and drag it to the book page. On the right-hand side of the book you can add your text (see Image 2).

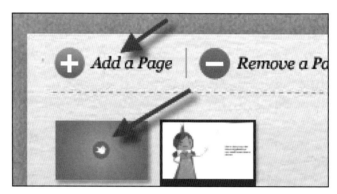

2: choosing image and adding text

6   You can add as many pages as you wish by clicking 'add page' in the bottom control bar. After you have finished, you can add a cover for your book by clicking on the cover field in the bottom control bar (see Image 3).

3: adding pages/adding cover

7   After you have finished with your story, click 'Save' in the right top corner. Then click 'Menu' and 'Publish this storybird'. Do not worry, the general settings in Storybird are private. You will be asked to give your story a title.

8   You can then add a summary of your story and other relevant information. Then click 'Publish' (see Image 4).

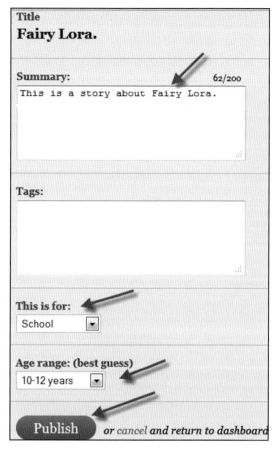

Title
Fairy Lora.

Summary: 62/200

This is a story about Fairy Lora.

Tags:

This is for:

School

Age range: (best guess)

10-12 years

Publish   or *cancel* **and return to dashboard**

4: adding relevant information (summary etc.)

9   In order to watch your story in full screen, click on 'Open' in the story. If you want to share the URL of your story, copy the address in the browser bar.

in class

Lead-in

1   Tell your students that they are going to create a picture story. They can write about anything they like.

2   Present your picture story.

Online

1   Tell your students to register at www.storybird.com, and help them with the registration process.

2   Show your students how to work with Storybird.

2.7 Arty stories

3   Give your students plenty of time to create their own stories.

Note: It is important that students can choose any templates and can write any story they like.

4   Walk around in class and help your students.

follow-up

1   In the next lesson, let students present their stories.

Learn more
http://storybird.com/tour/

2.8

Prezi for Prezident!

Application:	Prezi, www.prezi.com; lets you and your students create highly visual, dynamic and non-linear presentations. Prezi is a reasonable alternative to existing presentation software.
Similar application:	Popplet, www.popplet.com (see Activity 3.6)
Focus:	creating dynamic, non-linear presentations
Level:	elementary–intermediate.
Age:	any, though under-13s may not provide personal information to the site
Time:	depends on presentation
ICT skills:	browsing, typing, copying & pasting, uploading
Equipment:	computer lab OR single computer

Do It Yourself

1   Go to prezi.com/pricing/, scroll down and click on the Students & Teachers button, then register for an Edu Enjoy account. You will need to prove that you are a teacher by giving your school's name, email address, geographical location and website. The sign up procedure involves an email being sent to you.

   Note: For this activity, only Prezi's basic features are provided. For a detailed overview of Prezi's features, visit the tutorials/ workshops at http://prezi.com/learn.

2   In the 'Your Prezis' menu, click 'New prezi'.

3   Give your presentation a title and description. (In our example, we will prepare a presentation about the use of the past tense simple.) Then click 'Create new prezi'.

4   Now you can choose between various templates. Double-click on the template 'Explain a topic'.

5   Now you can see the template on the screen. To start editing, you may need to click 'start editing' in the bottom right corner, or you may be able to edit straight away.

6   If you see a window offering you help, close it (i.e. click on the X).

7   To edit the headline, double-click in the central circle. 'Edit' mode opens. Now type in the title of your headline (in our case 'The Past Tense Simple') (see Image 1).

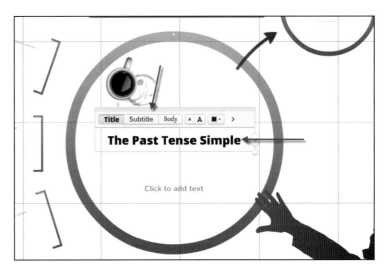

1: typing in the headline

8   If you want to change the headline font, click on the title once and use the layout buttons '+' (maximise), '-' (minimise) and the wheel to rotate the text (see Image 2)

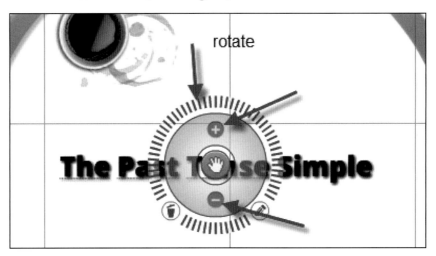

2: adjusting layout

9   In order to delete objects (texts, signs etc.), click on the item once, and then 'Delete' on your keyboard.

10   To start with your first slide, double-click on the any field and type in your title. If you want to add more information below your title, double-click in a blank space below the title. A new field appears.

11 Again, you can adjust size etc. as in Step 8.

Note: To zoom into and out of the whole presentation, click '+' or '-' in the control bar on the right.

12 When you want to go on to the next slide, double-click on a blank space anywhere and repeat from Step 7.

13 You can add videos and images. Click on the item/space where you want to add media. Then click on 'Image' in the control bar on top. (see Image 3).

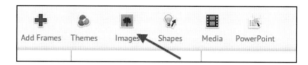

3: control bar

14 Add an image by uploading one from your computer or adding a URL link to the image. You can also use the built-in Google search to upload an image. The image will appear. Choose a picture you like. Then click "OK" to add the picture to your Prezi. You can adjust size etc. (as in Step 8). You can also drag the image to wherever you want it to go.

15 Create as many slides as you wish (as in Steps 7–11).

16 After you have finished, you can decide on the sequence (i.e. path) of your presentation. Click on 'Edit Path' in the control bar in the top left corner. Either you accept the order shown in the template or, to change the order, click on the red crosses (in the control bar; they will appear when you hover over the slides) and then click on the titles in the order you want them to appear.

17 If you want to preview your Prezi, click on the 'Present' button in the top left corner. Then start and navigate your presentation with the 'right' (forward) and 'left' (back) buttons on your keyboard.

18 To stop your presentation, click 'Esc.'.

Note: Prezi presentations (free account) can only be presented **online**.

in class

Lead-in

1 Set up a projector and show your Prezi presentation to your students.

2.8 Prezi for Prezident!

Variation 1 - Collaborative Prezi
You can also use Prezi as a collaboration tool. You can invite students to create a new presentation together in groups or modify/adapt an existing one. Click on the icon with the two heads, then in the top control bar (see Image 4).

4: starting to collaborate

Online
1   Then copy the link and give it to your students (see Image 5).

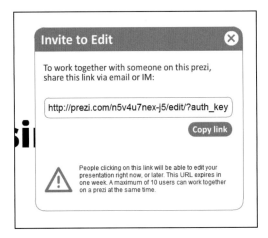

5: copy the link

Your students will need a Prezi account as well. A maximum of 10 people can work on a presentation collaboratively. You can form groups of 2-3 people.

Variation 2 - Grammar Prezis
Students could create their own grammar Prezis. In groups of 3, one student is responsible for providing the grammar notes (that can be simply copied from the textbook), another student for looking for examples of those usages online and copying/pasting them, and the third student for finding and placing videos from YouTube.

2.8 Prezi for Prezident!

Variation 3 – Student Prezentation
Invite your students to use Prezi for their presentations in class.

Learn more
http://prezi.com/learn/

2.9

Been there, done that …

Application:	Tripline, www.tripline.net; lets you and your students create timelines with descriptions and photos about places you were in.
Similar application:	Capzles, www.capzles.net (see Activity 2.2); Scribblemaps www.scribblemaps.com
Focus:	reconstructing trips, excursions etc. on Google Maps
Level:	pre-intermediate–advanced.
Age:	13+ only
Time:	90 minutes
ICT skills:	browsing, typing, copying & pasting, uploading
Equipment:	computer lab OR single computer
Preparation:	When your students go on an excursion or field trip – with either you or another teacher – encourage them to take pictures and take notes that they can use for digital presentations.

Do It Yourself

1   Register at www.tripline.net. You have to do this in order to use the site (click 'Sign up without Facebook').

2   In order to work with Tripline in class, we recommend trying out a map yourself.

3   Click on 'Create a new map' in the top control bar.

4   Type in the required fields (see Image 1). (You may also see an extra option: Start from my home location.) Here we'll be making a tripline about a trip to Vienna.

Re: the Visibility options, if you choose 'private', only registered users with the correct URL can watch your tripline. If you choose 'public', unregistered users can also watch the video.
Then click 'Create My Map'.

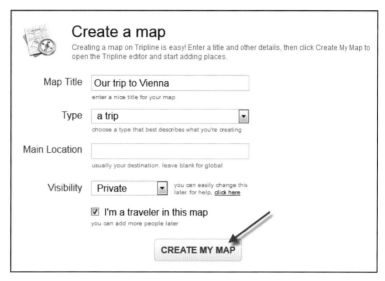

1: typing in details

5 A world map will appear. Scroll down and, on the right-hand side, enter some basic facts about the trip (see Image 2). You have an option to change your mind about the visibility if you choose.

2: basic facts about the trip

6   Next, start your tripline with a starting point (in this case CDG Airport Paris). Under 'Add places' on the left, type the place (e.g. "Airport CDG") and click 'Search'. You can zoom in (click 'Zoom', see Image 3) in order to get a more detailed view of the place. If you want to zoom out, click on the '-' (minus sign) button in the map. Then click 'Add place' (see Image 3).

3: finding places

7   You can insert the date when you departed from Paris (see Image 4). Click on the calendar to set the date.

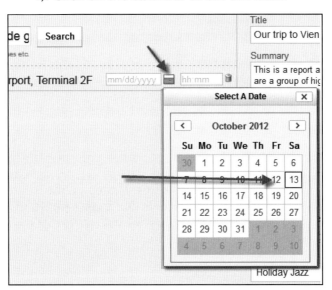

4: adding date

8   Then you can add other details, such as description and presentation mode. Hover over the destination and a pencil button will appear; click and some fields open beneath. Now you can write a short text about each destination. Set 'Player Animation' onto 'Slideshow' (see Image 5). Then click 'Update'.

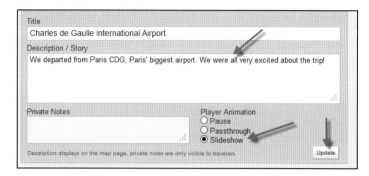

5: adding relevant information

9   Now search for your next destination (in our case, 'Vienna Airport') and repeat Steps 6–8 (see Image 6).

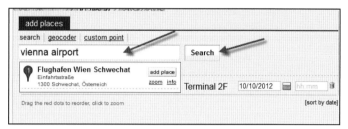

6: adding destinations

10 To add more destinations, repeat Steps 6–9 (adding dates, short texts, sights, restaurants etc.)

11 After you have entered all your destinations, click 'Save Map' at the bottom.

12 Now you can add photos to your destination. Hover over the destination and click on the 'Photo camera' sign, choose 'FlickR' (for copyright-free photos), click 'search', double-click on a photo of your choice (in our case a photo of CDG Airport Paris) – (see Image 7) and click 'Add photos'. You can repeat this step with all the other destinations.

7: adding photos

13 When you have finished, you can watch your tripline by clicking on the big ▶ (play) button (see Image 8) in the middle of the map. If you want to share/present your link, click on 'Share' (see Image 8), and copy the link and distribute it to your students.

8: watching your tripline

14 To edit your maps, click on 'My maps' in the top right corner.

in class

Lead-in

1 Tell your students that they will have the opportunity to make a short video about the excursion or field trip they went on with the class.

2   Show your Tripline video to your students. Then provide the link to your tripline so that they can watch the video several times.

Online

1   Show your students how to work with Tripline.

2   Then form groups and tell your students that they should create a similar video about a field trip, excursion etc. Give plenty of time (60 minutes minimum), and walk around and help your students.

Follow-up

1   In the next lesson students can present their videos.

2   Tell your students to post the URLs of their triplines into a backchannel like Todaysmeet (see Activity 3.4). Each group can watch a video by another group and add a comment (type in the URL of the video and click 'comment' below the video).

Variation – 'The must-see-sights tour of ...'
If you are looking at a particular country in your English lesson, ask your students to create a tripline about this country including descriptions of the most important sights/venues.

Learn more
http://tripline.net/explore

2.10 Ka-ching!

Application:	Wordsift, www.wordsift.com; lets you and your students visualise texts in various ways (images, contextualised sentences, tag clouds etc.).
Similar application:	Wordle, www.wordle.net (see Activity 2.1)
Focus:	create tag clouds, contextualised sentences and a thesaurus at once
Level:	intermediate
Age:	any
Time:	50 minutes
ICT skills:	browsing, typing, copying & pasting
Equipment:	computer lab, projector, speakers, images related to money, post-it notes
Preparation:	1 Go to www.youtube.com and find a video of 'Ka-Ching!' by Shania Twain.
	2 Record the link to use in the lesson.

Top Tip: Use a YouTube Channel (see Activity 1.4) to save your video and any others you want – e.g., the wacky song 'Money', from *Cabaret*. In the lesson, all you'll need to do in order to display all your videos is log into your Channel and click.

Do It Yourself

1 Go to www.wordsift.com and paste the lyrics of 'Ka-Ching!' into the box. There is no need to register. Click 'Sift' (see Image 1).

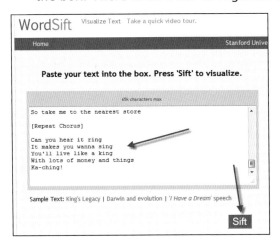

1: pasting text and sifting

2.10 Ka-ching!

2   What you get is an extensive visualisation of the text, which can be used to help students to understand key words in it (see Image 2).

In the top section, you find the words which frequently appear in the text. On the left are images associated with the word selected (here it's 'want'). On the right is a thesaurus, to help find synonyms.

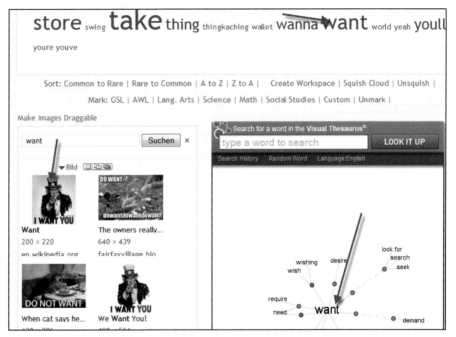

2: visualisation

3   You can click any word in the top box to find out more about its meaning; not only does the clicked word appear in the visual thesaurus, but also, on scrolling down, you will find the word (in Image 3 we've used 'spend') in context.

2.10 Ka-ching!

Examples from Source

'Spend'

We live in a greedy little world-- That teaches every little boy and girl To earn as much as they can possibly-- Then turn around and Spend it foolishly Weve created us a credit card mess We spend the money the we dont possess Our religion is to go and blow it all So its shoppin every sunday at the mall All we ever want is more A lot more than we had before So take me to the nearest store Can you hear it ring It makes you wanna sing Its such a beautiful thing--ka-ching! Lots of diamond rings The happiness it brings Youll live like a king With lots of money and things When youre broke go and get a loan Take out another mortgage on your home Consolidate so you can afford To go and spend some more when You get bored [Lyrics from: http://www.lyricsfreak.com/s/shania+twain/ka+ching_20123828.html] All we ever want is more A lot more than we had before So take me to the nearest store Can you hear it ring It makes you wanna sing Its such a beautiful thing--ka-ching! Lots of diamond rings The happiness it brings Youll live like a king With lots of money and things Lets swing Dig deeper in your pocket Oh, yeah, ha Come on I know youve got it Dig deeper in your wallet Oh All we ever want is more A lot more than we had before So take me to the nearest store Can you hear it ring It makes you wanna sing Its such a beautiful thing--ka-ching! Lots of diamond rings The happiness it brings Youll live like a king With lots of money and things Can you hear it ring It makes you wanna sing Youll live like a king With lots of money and things Ka-ching!.

3: 'spend' in context

4 For the lead-in activity, prepare 5–10 images related to money (e.g. a currency note, Wall Street, financial crisis, shopping mall, a millionaire etc.)

Top Tip: Use www.flickr.com for copyright-free, royalty-free images.

in class

Lead-in

1 Start the lesson by posting your money-related images, one by one, on the board. After putting up each image, ask students what they can see in the picture.

2 After you have put up all the images, tell your students to pick up some post-it notes (so if there are five images on the board, they should take five post-it notes).

3 Working individually, they stick up short notes/associations next to each image on the board.

4 When your students have finished, tell them to have a look at their classmates' associations.

5 Discuss the associations as a class.

Online

1 Show the video 'Ka-Ching!' to the students.

2 After the video ask them what they could see and/or understand.

3 Then tell the students to go to www.wordsift.com. Tell them to find the lyrics of 'Ka-Ching!' on the internet, copy & paste them into the field in Wordsift, and click 'Sift'.

4 Show them the three ways Wordsift can help them find more about the meanings of words.

5 Then, tell your students to browse through Wordsift clicking various words in order to see the main message of the text. You can also hand out questions like:
   • Which words appear most frequently in the text? Are there any reasons for that?
   • Find synonyms for the words 'wanna', 'spend' etc.
   • Name 10 words you already knew from the list.
   • Name 5 words that were new to you!
   • What's the main message of this song?

Follow-up

For homework, tell your students to pick their favourite song. They should paste the lyrics into Wordsift and answer the questions in Step 5 above.

Variation 1 – Famous speeches
For students at higher levels, you can use Wordsift for famous/historical speeches.

Variation 2 – News stories
Students can use Wordsift with news stories.

Variation 3 – My text – visualised
Tell your students to paste their homework task, when completed, into Wordsift. With one click, they see which words they frequently use. If some words have been used too often, they can use a thesaurus to replace those words.

Top Tip: Before doing this task, it can be helpful to practise using a traditional thesaurus in class to help students understand that not all synonyms can be used in a similar context.

2.11 Australia is QReat!

Application:	GoQr, http://goqr.me; easily creates QR codes (Quick Response codes). QR codes come in the form of a ciphered image; smartphones can be used to decipher the codes on certain documents, products, links etc.
Similar application:	Kaywa, http://qrcode.kaywa.com
Focus:	creating QR (Quick Response) codes
Level:	pre-intermediate
Age:	any
Time:	30 minutes
ICT skills:	browsing, typing, copying & pasting
Equipment:	smartphones with internet access (both you and students) and a QR-code reader (to find this in either App Store or Android Market, type 'QR reader'). NB: It is often the case that not every student owns a smartphone with internet access. Check before planning your lesson that enough students have internet smartphones to allow students who do not own one to work with those who do.
Preparation:	Print out several more QR codes with various questions, links etc. (see, e.g., Image 1). Just before the lesson, put these up around the classroom as QR stations for Lead-in Step 2. To learn how to make QR code questions, see the Do it Yourself section.

1: a sample code (Source: FlickR, nickj365 (Creative Commons))

2.11 Australia is QReat!

1   Go to http://goqr.me. There is no need to register.

2   Think of various questions on a certain topic; for this example, we are going to create a quiz about Australia. We suggest you type your questions into a word processing program, then copy & paste them into the GoQR 'Your text' box and click 'Open' (see Images 2 and 3).

Australia Quiz – Class 4B – Mr Strasser   write the text into a word processing software and copy it

Welcome to the great Australia quiz.

Try to answer the questions on a sheet of paper. Good luck ☺

1.   What's the capital of Australia?
2.   What's the largest state in Australia?
3.   What's another name for "Uluru"?

2: typing your text into a word processing program

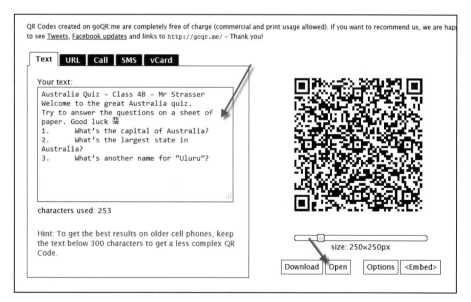

3: pasting your text into GoQR and clicking 'Open'

3   A QR code will appear. Leave it open on your computer screen or, if necessary, print it.

4   On your smartphone, open your QR reader and move your phone about in front of the QR code on screen or on paper, just as if you were taking a picture, until the application on your phone recognises the code. This is what you will see then (see Image 4):

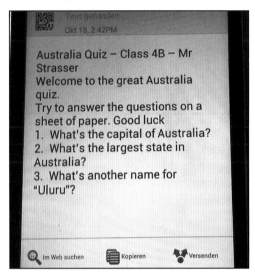

4: the questions transferred to your smartphone

5   Find an image of a QR code and print it or save it, ready to project in class.

Lead-in

1   Put up your QR code on the board or project it onto the wall. Ask students if they know codes like this. Ask them if they have already seen this code on commercial posters or billboards in the tube, at the bus station etc.

2   Have them look at your QR stations around the room.

3   Then tell them that you are going to work with QR codes in the classroom.

Online

1   Tell your students that you are going to play 'Treasure Hunt Australia'. Your students need their smartphones with internet access, a QR reader (if they haven't got one, see 'Equipment') and a sheet of paper and a pen. Tell them to work in pairs or groups of 3.

2   Show them how a QR reader works. Then let students move around in class in order to visit all the QR stations (in this activity, the QR code questions, links, etc. should be related to the topic of Australia).

3   After your students have finished, discuss the answers as a class.

   Top Tip: Allow students to do research on their smartphones.

Follow-up

Tell your students that they should imagine that they are on holiday in Australia for two weeks. They should write a postcard to their best friend including the following things:
• Introduction
• What you have done so far (sights, adventures etc.)
• What you are planning to do (sights, trips etc.)
• What you liked best on this trip
• What you didn't really like on this trip
• Greetings.
After writing the assignment with a word processing program, they should paste their text into a QR generator and print out the code. You collect the codes and read the stories. Then you can give feedback, using a QR code again, handing it back to the student.

Variation 1 – The extra bit
If you are using Powerpoint or similar presentation software in class, you can use QR codes to provide links with additional info to a certain topic, e.g. if you are giving a presentation on 'school systems in the UK', you can create a QR code directing the students to useful websites. The big advantage here is that students do not have to write down long URLs.

Variation 2 – QRs on a handout
When you prepare handouts for classroom use, e.g. on past simple vs. progressive, you can add QR codes directing the students to websites offering similar exercises online.

Variation 3 – Scavenger hunt
If this variation is acceptable in your school, post QR codes around the school building(s) before the lesson. In class, give your students the first QR code, with an instruction where to go next to pick up the next QR code. E.g. *Go to the place where you can always smell what's for lunch.* (Solution: *cafeteria*).

Credits: @hamtra

Top tip: You could also hide some QR codes outside the school (school yard etc.) if this is allowed.

Variation 4 – The film of the book
When reading a book in class, print out QR codes with the link to the film trailer and put them into every copy of the book.

Variation 5 - Assignments

Type instructions for homework and create a QR code. Display the code on your screen or IWB and have students scan the code.

2.12 Funky Pic Dic style

Application:	Animoto, www.animoto.com; turns your videos or images into impressive presentations with music and recorded sound.
Similar application:	Stupeflix, www.stupeflix.com; Photovisi, www.photovisi.com (cf. Activity 2.5)
Focus:	create multimedia presentations
Level:	all levels (this example is elementary–pre-intermediate)
Age:	any, so long as under 13s access the site only via your educator's account (see Do It Yourself 1, Top Tip).
Time:	20 minutes
ICT skills:	browsing, typing, copying & pasting
Equipment:	computer, speakers, projector
Preparation:	Think of some animals that you and some of your students can mime in front of the class.

Do It Yourself

1 Go to www.animoto.com and register. Animoto is free, and you can use it to create 30-second clips.

   Top Tip: As a teacher, go to www.animoto.com/education and you will get an educator's Animoto Plus account for free, giving you six months of unlimited recording time, and allowing up to 50 of your students to get a six-months-plus account as well by using an entry code! *NB the process of applying for this type of account may involve a wait of several weeks.*

2 Then click 'Create Video' in the top right corner.

3 Then choose a template/style you like (see Image 1) and click 'Create video'.

2.12 Funky Pic Dic style

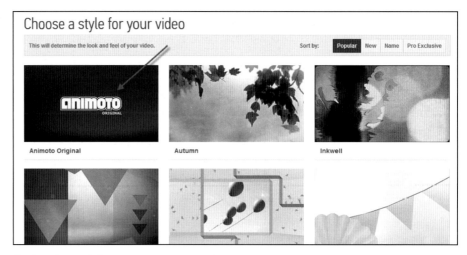

1: choosing a style

4   Then click 'Add Pics & Vids'. Now you can choose to upload pictures from your computer, from Facebook, FlickR, Picasa etc. (see Image 2) that you want to teach to your students. In this example, we'll be choosing some pictures relating to animal words.

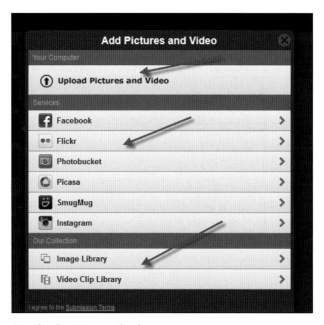

2: uploading images / videos

5   Click 'Image Library' then pick the 'Animals' collection. To pick a range of images from this page, use Shift-click; for different ones here and there, use Ctrl-click (see Image 3). Then click on 'Add xx items'.

3: using Ctrl-click to pick more than one picture

6   Now change the music; you can pick the type of music and then an actual song (see Image 4).

4: picking a song

7   Then add text. You can start with the title of the presentation and some additional information (see Image 5). Then click 'Save'.

2.12 Funky Pic Dic style

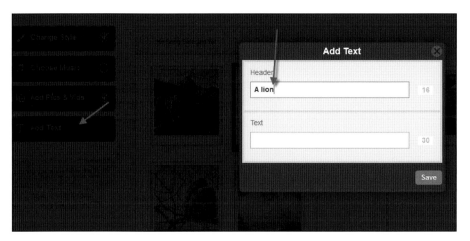

5: adding text

8   Then add more pages; title each one with the name of an animal and drag it into position beside its image (see Image 6).

6: adding pages and moving them into position

After you have put your images and texts in order, click 'Preview Video' or 'Skip and Produce'. Wait for a few minutes, then click the 'Play' button to watch your video.

9   Copy the URL above the video for classroom use.

in class **Lead-in**

1   Mime one of your animals, and let your students guess which one it is. Ask the student who guessed the animal to provide a sentence with this animal in context, e.g. 'The lion is the king of the animals.'

2   Ask this student to come out to the front. Whisper another animal into the student's ear, for him/her to mime it. The other students guess the animal and come up with a contextualised sentence. Repeat this procedure a couple of times.

Online

1   Now tell your students to relax.

2   Tell them that you are going to watch a visual picture dictionary.

3   Play the Animoto video.

4   After the video, ask one student to list as many animals as he or she can remember.

   Note: Animoto is a good tool for the multi-sensory learner.

Variation 1 – Photo story
Your students can use Animoto in order to create a photo story. They can either use pictures from the extensive Animoto collection or take photos on their mobile phones and add them to their Animoto story.

Variation 2 – Visual input
As an alternative to direct lecturing, the teacher can use Animoto to give topic-related input to the class (e.g. a presentation about London, historical events, various lexical categories like food, housing etc.)

Learn more
http://animoto.com/sample-videos

2.13 Show me what you like!

Application:	screenr, www.screenr.com; a simple web-based screen recorder that lets you and your students record video tutorials or screencasts.
Similar application:	Screencastle, http://screencastle.com
Focus:	producing screencasts/video tutorials
Level:	pre-intermediate–advanced
Age:	13+ only
Time:	60 minutes
ICT skills:	browsing, typing, copying & pasting
Equipment:	computer lab, headset (mandatory), projector, speakers, Facebook or Twitter or Google+ or WindowsLive or Yahoo-account

Do It Yourself

1   Go to www.screenr.com. You need to log on using your Twitter, Facebook, Google+ account. NB This application uses Java. *We suggest that you check which version of Java your computer is running. The distributors, Sun Microsystems, strongly advise that if your computer has a version older than Version 7 Update 5, you completely remove the earlier version asap and replace it with 7:5. (Java is used not just for screenr, but also for (probably several) other applications in your computer.)*

2   Open some documents and websites that you find interesting. Make sure you have your microphone plugged in (this could be a stand-alone model, or in a headset or in a webcam).Click 'Launch screen recorder now'.

3   The recording frame that appears allows you to select an area on your screen that you would like to record visually. This area can be in the document or website you've chosen. Move its window alongside the screenr one, then drag the recording frame across by clicking on its edge, and resize it by using the handles in the corners (see Image 1).

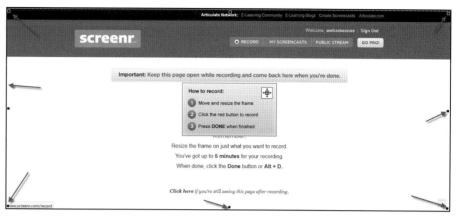

1: the resizing handles

4   After you have chosen your area, click the Record button at the bottom left corner (see Image 2). Here, I would add a "Top Tip": a key feature when recording is using ALT+D to pause. This makes it easy to take your time recording a screencast and makes sure you get it right first time.

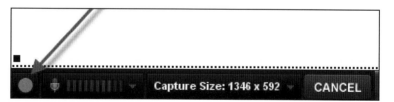

2: the record button

5   You can move on to other interesting and striking images and content on your screen, and comment on everything you see.

   Top Tip 1: When recording speech, try not to go too fast, especially with explanations. While for you certain things may seem to be logical, often for the viewer they are not. So speak slowly and clearly, and explain carefully.

   Top Tip 2: Here are some aspects of a favourite website which might be interesting:
   • General content (news, celebrities, sports etc.)
   • Layout (colours, images, fonts etc.)
   • Media (videos, audio, images etc.)
   • Communication (forums, chats etc.)
   • Different sections.

6   When you have finished, go back to your screenr page and click 'Done'.

7   Then type a short description of your screencast and then click 'Publish' (see Image 3). If you haven't yet registered or logged in, you will need to do so now. You'll need to wait for the same length of time as it took to make your recording, then you can click 'Play'.

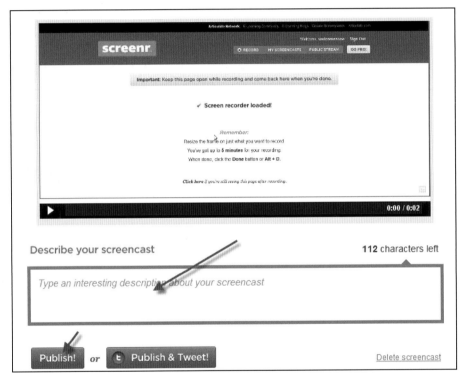

3: describing and publishing your screencast

8   After your videocast has been created, you have several publishing options:
   - Embedding the video into a homepage, blog, or learning platform
   - Providing the URL link (probably the easiest way to show the video to your students)
   - Downloading the video onto your computer etc (see Image 4).

2.13 Show me what you like!

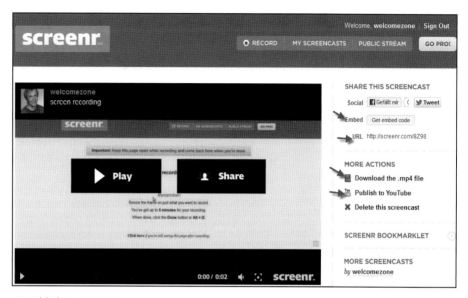

4: publishing options

Lead-in

1 Start the lesson by asking your students the following questions:
   - What makes a good homepage in general?
   - Which content are you interested in? (news, sports, gossip etc.)
   - Do you often watch videos, look at images etc.?
   - Do you often communicate on your favourite websites?

   Collect the ideas on the board in a mindmap, or use Wordle (see Activity 2.1) to type in the students' suggestions and create a tag cloud.

Online

1 Show your presentation of your favourite website to the students. Tell them that you are going to produce one as well.

2 Show them how to create a screencast with screenr.

3 Now tell them to produce a presentation about their favourite website in pairs/groups using screenr and a headset with a microphone. Project the aspects they should include in their presentation:
   - General content (news, celebrities, sports etc.)
   - Layout (colours, images, fonts etc.)
   - Media (videos, audio, images etc.)
   - Communication (forums, chats etc.)

   Top Tip: If the computers in the lab do not have microphones, you can tell the students to present their favourite website by using the mouse to indicate interesting aspects. Alternatively, you may ask the students to make recordings of 2–5 minutes.

That way, if there are not enough microphones for everyone, they can be easily shared; the students who have finished their recordings can take the microphones to the front so that other students can help themselves

4   Walk around and help your students with vocabulary etc.

5   After your students have finished, let them present their websites on a projector. Encourage the other students to give feedback and ask questions.

Follow-up

1   Tell students that they should provide the URL of their screencast to another group. This group can add feedback to their screencast by typing in text below the video (see Image 5).

5: adding feedback to a screencast

Variation 1 – Technical input in computer lab – the rest at home
If you think that it might be a better idea to let students produce their screencast at home, do the tutorial on how to work with screenr in the computer lab (and let them start working) and tell them to finish/ produce their screencast at home as an assignment.

Variation 2 – Tutorials
Screenr is an ideal tool to produce tutorials about applications, the use of websites and many other procedures. Not only can you as the teacher provide tutorials relevant to your EFL lessons, but also the students can produce tutorials on things they are good at. Encourage your students to produce tutorials about video games, software programs, websites etc. Tell them to produce the screencasts in English.

Variation 3 – Feedback
Tell your students to send you their essays via email. Use screenr or other video captions applications to correct the texts with the Comment tool of your word processor, and also use audio (to tell the students what you like or what needs to be improved). Then send the videocast to your students.

CHAPTER 3
COLLABORATION

3.1 'Once upon a time …'

Application:	PiratePad, http://www.piratepad.net; lets students write texts collaboratively in real time.
Similar application:	Typewithme, www.typewith.me; Edupad, http://www.edupad.ch; Titanpad, http://titanpad.com/; Primarywall, www.primarywall.com
Focus:	collaborative text writing in real time
Level:	beginner–advanced
Age:	any – registration not required
Time:	30 minutes
ICT skills:	typing, chatting
Equipment:	computer lab, one computer per 2 students; if necessary, one computer can be shared between up to 6 students

Do It Yourself

1   Go to http://www.piratepad.net.

2   Click on 'The PiratePad greets you'.

3   In the URL bar, delete the grey text after the slash (/) and type a name of your own (see Image 1, where we've typed 'mind-the-app1). Then press the Enter key.

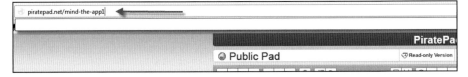

1: giving your pad its own URL

4   PiratePad asks you to create your pad. Click 'Yes, please create the pad' (see Image 2).

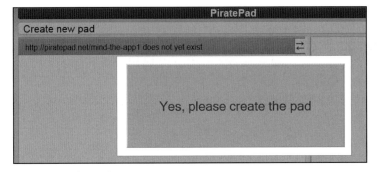

2: creating the pad

5   In the box at top right, enter your name or a nickname (here, we've used 'teacher', see Image 3).

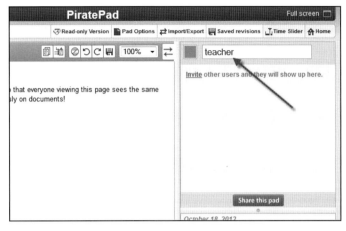

3: typing in your nickname

6   Delete the text in the big box and type your general instructions to your students, followed by your text-writing instructions. In our example (see Image 4), students are being invited to write a fairy tale together.

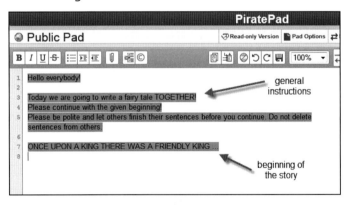

4: drafting general and text-writing instructions

7   Copy your URL and save it ready for the lesson.

in class

Lead-in

1   Draw a mindmap on the board and ask your students for words that link a text (e.g. *and*, *in addition*, *but* etc.). You can also collect typical fairytale words/phrases (*Once upon a time ...*', *princess*, *sword* etc.) depending on the level of your students.

Online

1   Tell the students that they are going to write a text together in real time. Ask students to work in pairs (two students sharing one computer), or bigger groups if need be (and see note on next page).

2   Discuss the Netiquette (see App Toolkit at the start of this chapter) with them.

3   Write your URL on the board (here, it's piratepad.net/mind-the-app1). Tell the students to type it into the browser of their computer. Then they type their name into the box (see Image 5).

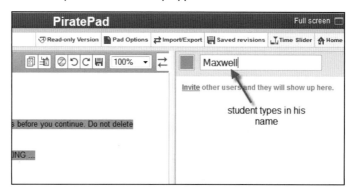

5: student types name into pad

4   Then, following the netiquette rules, students can now start writing a fairy tale together in real time (see Image 6).

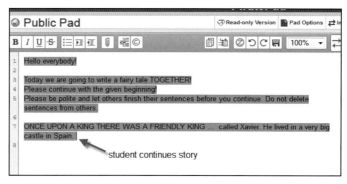

6: writing process with pad

Set a time limit of about 20–30 minutes for your students to write.

Note: If you don't have enough computers for several small groups, here are some alternative ideas:
*   On each available computer, open more than one pad and number its URL, so that, e.g., the first 6 students use piratepad.net/mind-the-app1, the second 6 students use piratepad.net/mind-the-app2.

- All the groups work together on a single pad, but there is only one 'writer' (i.e. a person who types in the story from each group).

Variation 1 – Brainstorming

PiratePad can be used for brainstorming sequences with students at all levels. Write the topic you would like your students to brainstorm. Students then write down all the things they associate with it. After some time, discuss the findings from the pad.

Variation 2 – giving feedback

You can also use PiratePad for evaluation purposes; your students can use it to give you feedback on your lessons.

More PiratePad functions
- You can change the appearance of the text (see Image 7).

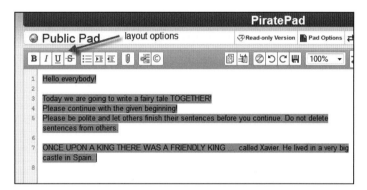

7: change the appearance of a text

- You can save the text at intervals (see Image 8).

8: saving a text

- You can use the Timeslider function: click 'Timeslider' (see Image 8 again), then click on the triangle 'play' button (see Image 9) in order to present the full writing process. You can press 'Pause' (with inverted commas) at any time. This function is very useful if you want to talk about some interesting sections of the text.

'Once upon a time ...'

9: time slider

- You can also export the text in order to print it out or save it on your computer (see Image 10).

10: export the text

Follow-up/ homework

1 Tell your students to read their collaboratively produced fairy tale again at home.

2 At home, students should cut out or print images representing the fairy tale.

3 In class, pick some students to present their fairy tale with their images.

3.2

Webpage juror

Application:	Markup, www.markup.io; lets you draw on any webpage with a variety of tools to express your thoughts, make a point or simply add comments. Collaborative website analysis made easy!
Similar application:	Bounce App, www.bounceapp.com
Focus:	webpage analysis
Level:	upper intermediate–advanced
Age:	any – registration not required
Time:	40+ minutes
ICT skills:	browsing, typing
Equipment:	computer lab (OR students can work at home), green/red post-its

Preparation:

1 For Online Step 5, check how the students will be able to send a link from the computer they are using to their classmates' computers and yours in the lab.

2 Get a supply of red and green post-it notes.

Do It Yourself

1 Find some websites you want your students to read and analyse.

2 Copy the website URLs and paste them into a document; you will need to give the links to your students in class.

   Top Tip: you can also use a backchannelling application like Todaysmeet (Activity 3.4) or Piratepad (Activity 3.1).

3 Ensure your browser has a bookmarks toolbar visible. (If not, you can normally right-click in the header area of your browser and, in the dropdown list, tick 'Bookmarks Toolbar'.)

4 Go to www.markup.io.

5 Click on the icon in the field 'Get Markup'; hold the left mouse button down, and drag it into the bookmarks bar of your browser, then release the mouse button (see Image 1).

3.2 Webpage juror

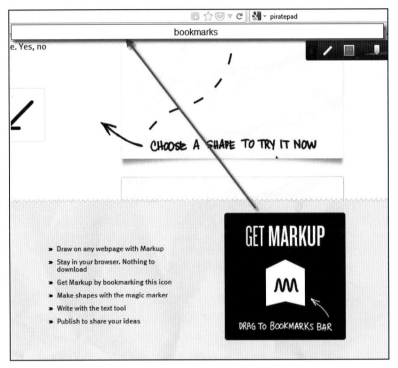

1: saving Markup in your bookmarks toolbar

6   Now there should be a bookmark called 'Markup' in your bookmarks toolbar (see Image 2).

2: Markup in your bookmarks toolbar.

7   Open a website you also want your students to analyse. In our case, we will use my Web 2.0 learning blog, www.learning-reloaded.com.

8   Click on the 'Markup' button in your bookmarks bar (see Image 3).

3.2 Webpage juror

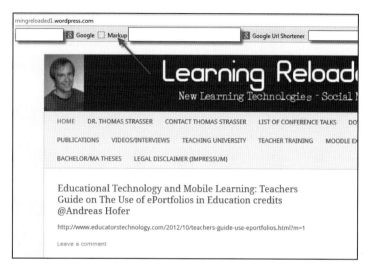

3: starting the Markup app

9 A Markup toolbar will open in the top right corner of your screen (see Image 4).

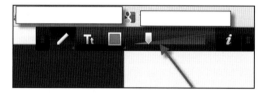

4: Markup toolbar

10 Now you are ready to start analysing and can draw and post comments on this website.

11 In order to mark or highlight certain features of a website, click on the 'pencil' (and choose the shape). If you want to add comments to certain parts of the site, click on the 'Tt-button'. If you want to draw on the site, click on the 'square' and choose a colour (see Image 5).

5: various settings in Markup

12 For example: you have found some useful links on the website and you want to add some comments. First click on the pencil icon, then its circle tool, and circle the link you want to highlight; then click the 'Tt-button' and write your comment (see Image 6).

3.2 Webpage juror

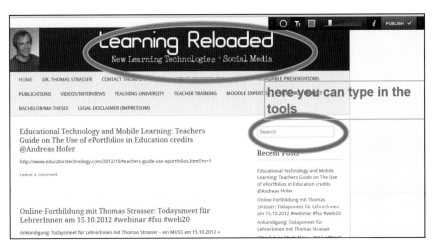

6: adding comments and highlighting passages

13 After you have finished your analysis, you can publish the link and send it to your students (click 'Publish'). (NB When you select the link to copy it, its appearance changes slightly.) They can open the link and insert additional comments, in a different colour, if they wish, before sending it on (see Image 7).

7: create a link and send it to others

3.2 Webpage juror

in class

Lead-in

1 Ensure your red and green post-its are to hand.

2 Hold a short class discussion on the qualitative criteria for a website (see box on next page). Then ask your students to find as many as possible *do's* (write them on green post-its) and *don'ts* (on red post-its) concerning the design/content of your chosen website.

Online

1 Tell your students that they are going to be Webpage Jurors and that they will read and analyse various websites.

2 Then explain Markup to your students. Let them try it out.

3 Now provide the links you have prepared and tell your students that they will be working with Markup (including all its tools), taking into consideration the criteria for a good website they discussed previously. They should comment on interesting things, appreciate nice ideas, give input for improvement (language mistakes etc.) or just highlight striking features of the websites.

4 After some time (depending on the number of websites to be analysed), tell your students how to publish their work and send the link with their comments to other classmates. The recipients should add some comments to the existing markup.

5 Finally, tell your students to send their Markup links to you.

Variation 1 – Treasure hunt

You can use Markup for a treasure hunt or webquest with students at all levels. Prepare a task sheet asking students to find certain information (e.g. *How much does a room cost in a youth hostel in London/Notting Hill? Where can you buy tickets for a New York Yankees game?*). Students try to find the answers, then mark it with Markup and publish the link. They can either send it to you or write it down on the task sheet.

Variation 2 – Language detective

With higher-level students, you can use websites that display some language errors. Tell the students that they are going to be language detectives and that they have to find the mistakes and 'arrest' them by highlighting them and correcting them with Markup's comment function.

Variation 3 – Real-time-annotator

Markup can also be used outside the computer lab. In the normal classroom (that has at least one computer and one projector), you can use Markup when showing videos (YouTube, BBC, CNN etc.), stopping at certain scenes and making annotations.

Criteria for a good website

What makes a 'good' website?

- Purpose: the site should have a clear purpose, e.g. to inform about a topic, to entertain, etc.
- Appearance: the site should use a variety of colours, should display contextualised images and videos, and should be generally appealing.
- Usability: a website should be user-friendly, i.e. should be easy to use and well-structured, and navigation should be intuitive.
- Language: depending on the purpose of the site, language should not be offensive, politically incorrect or vulgar. The site should not have language mistakes.
- Search function: the site should provide a search box in order for the user to look for certain terms/topics.

Follow-up

1 For homework, tell your students to find an example of a 'good' website and an example of a 'bad' website.

2 They should use Markup to make annotations based on the criteria discussed in Lead-in Step 2 (see the Criteria for a good website box on previous page).

3 Students then present their findings in class.

Top Tip: Shortcuts for Markup:

8: keyboard shortcuts

3.3 Chief analyst

Application: Crocodoc, http://personal.crocodoc.com/; allows students to work collaboratively on an online document, add comments, make suggestions etc.

Similar application: Showdocument, http://www.showdocument.com/

Focus: work collaboratively on online texts

Level: upper intermediate – advanced

Age: any if working without signing up, or 13+ if signing up; see Do It Yourself 1

Time: 60 minutes

ICT skills: making comments, highlighting, browsing

Equipment: computer lab OR single computer

Do It Yourself

1   You can upload a document into Crocodoc, but if you want to save files and manage them you'll need to sign up: http://personal.crocodoc.com/signup/.

2   Upload a document you would like your students to work on. In our example, we have used the famous 'Ich bin ein Berliner' speech by John F. Kennedy (see Image 1).

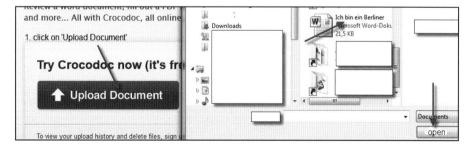

1: uploading files

3   Click on the uploaded file. In the top right corner click on 'Share'. Then you will be given a URL (see Image 2) that you can send.

3.3 Chief analyst

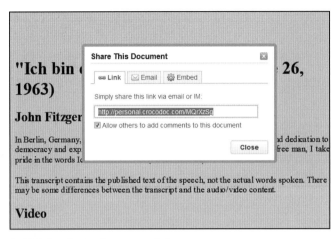

2: URL for the students to collaborate

Lead-in

1 In the computer lab, tell your students that they are to work in pairs and that they are the school's chief analysts. They will be analysing a speech taking the following aspects into account:
   - language (formal/informal, slang, technical etc.)
   - historical backgrounds
   - any striking features (metaphors, similes etc.)

Online

1 Then give your students the URL (see Image 3). If you want to see who has added/commented, tell your students aged 13+ to register for Crocodoc (although it is not obligatory).

2 Help your students with the basic features of Crocodoc.

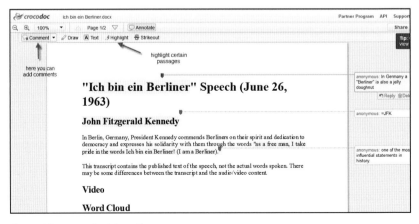

3: working on a text together

3   Now give your students time to work collaboratively on this speech. Tell them they must make all their comments in English!

4   At the end of the lesson, discuss the comments as a class, or let students finish off their analyses at home.

Variation 1 – Collaborative paraphrasing
With higher-level students, you can do some lexical exercises. Choose a topic and upload a vocabulary glossary. Students should now find synonyms and antonyms for these words; they can also try to paraphrase the words using Crocodoc.

Variation 2 – Are you serious!?
With higher-level students, you can upload various controversial statements about a certain topic. Invite students to comment on these statements and say whether they agree or not.

Variation 3 – Who was it?
Upload famous quotations, statements or parts of song lyrics. Let your students guess who wrote which statement, and tell them to write down how they came to that conclusion.

Variation 5 - Pic Dic
Upload specific pictures using Crocodoc. Invite students to label various parts of the image (e.g. body parts, parts of the computer, etc.)

3.4 Backchannelling

Application:	TodaysMeet, http://todaysmeet.com; helps students and teachers create a 'backchannel' for the lesson. A backchannel is a way for students to ask questions during the lessons in real time without interrupting you too much – or they can use the backchannel as a feedback tool.
Similar application:	Edupad, www.edupad.ch
Focus:	post questions during lessons
Level:	pre-intermediate–advanced
Age:	13+ only
Time:	1 teaching sequence
ICT skills:	browsing, typing
Equipment:	computer lab OR single computer; optional, a projector

Do It Yourself

1 Go to http://todaysmeet.com .

2 Name your room (the name must be a single word, no spaces) and adjust the settings (see Image 1).

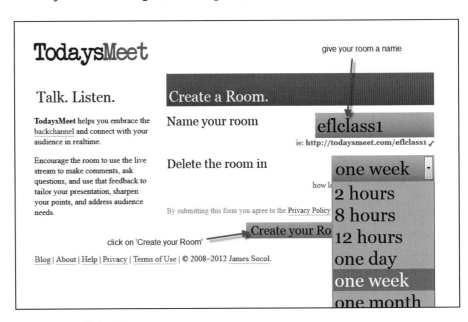

1: setting up TodaysMeet

3 Click on 'Create your Room' (see Image 1 again).

4 Copy the URL of your room (see Image 2) and save it for your class.

2: URL of your room

5 Type in your name and click 'Join' (see Image 3).

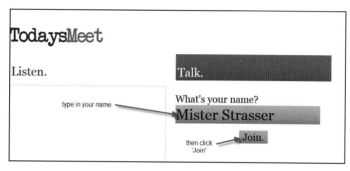

3: typing in your name

6 Then type a trial message into the Message box, and click 'Say' (see Image 4).

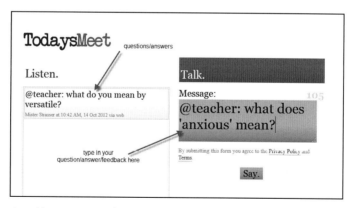

4: asking questions/giving answers

7 Your message moves into the 'Listen' box.

in class

Lead-in

1 Before starting the lesson in a computer lab, tell your students that, in this lesson, they will have the opportunity of asking questions online during the lesson. Explain to them that this can be an advantage, especially when asking questions that, although relevant, are not that urgent – and you can answer the question any time you want to.

Variation – At home

You can take advantage of TodaysMeet in a normal classroom as well. Tell your students to write down the link so they can post their opinion, then near the end of the lesson give them some time to write their feedback on a sheet of paper. At home, they type in it into TodaysMeet.

Online

1   Briefly explain how TodaysMeet works, and give the URL of your room to the students.

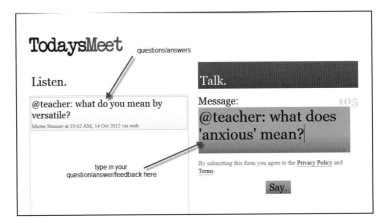

4: asking questions/giving answers

2   Let them open the URL, type their name and click 'Join'.

3   Start your lesson. The good thing about TodaysMeet is that it is not just you but also the students who can use the backchannel to give answers to each other to points raised.

4   Shortly before the end of the lesson, discuss the questions/answers, maybe using a projector.

Variation 1 – Long feedback

Invite your students to give feedback on your teaching performance; they should note everything they find effective. It would probably be a good idea to discuss some basic rules of feedback (e.g. give constructive feedback, use no swear words, offer reflective criticism and appreciation etc.).

Variation 2 – Short feedback

Invite your students to post just the things they liked best in your lesson, and to briefly explain why they like them.

Variation 3 – Quizmania

You can use TodaysMeet as a quiz generator. Tell your students to type in the URL of your backchannel and use it to ask various EFL-related questions. The first one who writes a correct answer gets a point.

Variation 4 – Vocabmania

Near the end of the lesson, post the words just learnt in L1, and have students translate them into L2. You can also provide the new vocabulary in L2 and ask students to contextualise the word (i.e. write it in a meaningful sentence).

Variation 5 – FAQs for an exam

You can also use TodaysMeet FAQ platform (Frequently Asked Questions). If students have any questions about an exam, they can use TodaysMeet to post the questions; not only you but also their classmates can respond to these.

Variation 6 – Presentation feedback

When students are giving presentations in the EFL lesson, you can invite them to use TodaysMeet to get feedback or take questions.

Variation 7 – Link provider

Invite students to post useful links (videos, grammar activities, texts etc.) on TodaysMeet.

3.5 Go vote!

Application:	Flisti, www.flisti.com; lets you easily create surveys and polls to use in the EFL lesson.
Similar application:	Easypolls, www.easypolls.net; Surveymonkey, www.surveymonkey.com, Polldaddy www.polldaddy.com
Focus:	create a poll
Level:	elementary–advanced
Age:	any – no registration required
Time:	10 minutes
ICT skills:	browsing, typing
Equipment:	computer lab, single computer, or 2-3 computers in class

Do It Yourself

1 Go to www.flisti.com

2 Create a poll (see Image 1)

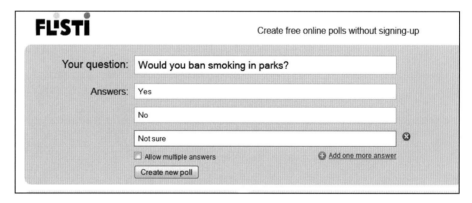

1: creating the poll

3 Click on 'Create new poll'.

4 Now your poll is ready (see Image 2). Copy the link in the URL bar at the top of the screen for your students.

3.5 Go vote!

2: finished poll

Online

1   Either at the beginning of a lesson to get a quick overview of the students' opinions, or at the end of a discussion, let students carry out the poll using your URL.

2   Discuss the results by clicking 'View results' (see Image 3).

3: viewing the results of a poll

Variation – Quiz

You can also use Flisti as a quiz generator to open and close the lesson. Prepare this by creating questions on grammatical, lexical, cultural etc. topics and then let students use it to guess the right answers.

3.5 Go vote!

Note: As this is only a short activity, we suggest you dedicate the rest of the lesson to internet-based activities (perhaps based on the survey topic) so that you do not go into the computer lab just for the survey.

3.6 Brainstorming deluxe

Application: Popplet, www.popplet.com; lets your students brainstorm and make a mindmap on any topic, using various media (videos, documents etc.)

Similar application: Mindmeister, www.mindmeister.com; Mind43, http://mind42.com; Scribblar www.scribblar.com

Focus: interactive and collaborative mindmapping/brainstorming

Level: intermediate–advanced

Age: 13+ only

Time: 60–90 minutes

ICT skills: browsing, typing, copying & pasting, uploading

Equipment: computer lab OR single computer

Preparation: In advance of the main lesson, spend a few minutes with your students to set up registration and collaboration. See Do It Yourself, Steps 10-14.

Do It Yourself

1 Register at www.popplet.com. You need to register in order to save your popplets (mindmaps).

2 Click on 'Make a new popplet'.

3 Give your popplet a name, pick a colour and click on 'Make it so!'. You may find a brief tutorial will run automatically.

4 By double-clicking on the blank grey screen (not on the tutorial window), a 'popple' (i.e. a mindmapping field) will be opened (see Image 1).

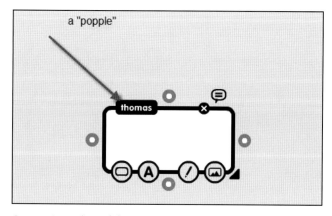

1: creating a 'popple'

5   Double-click in the 'popple' and type the topic in that you would like your students to brainstorm. In this case, it is the USA.

6   Now add one or two 'input fields' (i.e. concepts you associate with the USA) by clicking on the little dots next to the USA field (see Image 2).

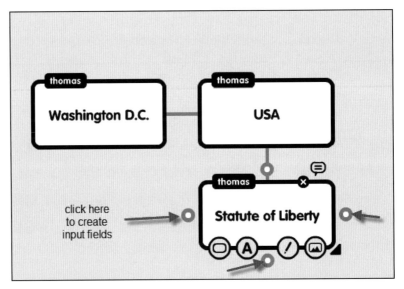

2: creating 'input fields'

7   In order to make the word in the main field (USA) bigger, click on it, then click on the 'A' beneath it, then on the larger size (see Image 3).

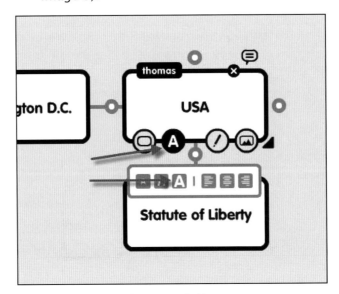

3: adjusting the size of the main field

3.6 Brainstorming deluxe

8   You can make this mindmap highly interactive by adding movies. In this example, we are adding a YouTube video to the topic field 'Statue of Liberty'. Click on the topic field 'Statue of Liberty', then on the right-hand icon beneath it, 'Upload things', then the 'YouTube' button. Type in your search query and double-click on the video you would like to add.

Note: If you don't already have a particular YouTube video in mind, it is advisable to open YouTube in a new browser tab and look for one. When you have found something suitable, type the keywords into the Popplet–YouTube search query. Now you have inserted a YouTube video into your mindmap.

9   You can also add photos or other media files from your computer.

10 Spend a preparatory period on registration. First, tell your students to register at www.popplet.com. Help them with the registration process.

11 Then distribute a list (either on paper or via email or a social networking site) for all students to write down their Popplet usernames and email addresses, and keep this aside for Step 13.

12 Then you must authenticate them to collaborate on your USA mindmap. Click on the 'wheel' near the top, click 'labs' and then 'popplet permissions' (see Image 4).

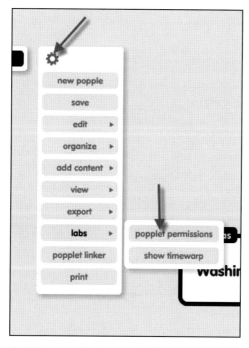

4: giving permission to collaborate

13 Then choose 'popples can be edited by any collaborator', 'OK'. Click 'share' in the top right corner , click 'add collaborator', search for your students using the list, and add them (see Image 5).

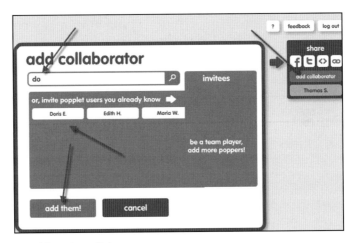

5: adding the collaborators

14 Finally click on 'share' and the link symbol in the right top corner and copy/write down the link for your students.

Additional features

1 In order to present the mindmap in a more dynamic way, click on the settings steering wheel (see Image 6) 'view', then 'presentation mode' or 'timewarp mode' (settings > labs > show timewarp).

2 You can also explore other options, such as:
- export mindmap as a pdf or a jpeg (Settings > Export)
- print mindmap (settings > print)

6: settings

3.6 Brainstorming deluxe

in class

1 Tell your students to log on to www.popplet.com.

2 Give your link to your students.

3 Before students start brainstorming, tell them that their answers should be short and intuitive. Also show them how to add various media like videos, images, documents etc.

4 Give your students plenty of time to brainstorm.

Follow-up

In the next lesson, discuss the brainstorming results with your students.

Variation 1 – Breaking the ice ...
Popplet can be perfect for introducing a new topic. Create a new mindmap and project it onto the wall in the classroom. Get the students to brainstorm about it. Invite them to come to the computer and type in their ideas. After the ideas have been collected, you can print them out for the students (see Additional Features on previous page).

Variation 2 – Beginner's visual dictionary
For students at lower levels, you can use Popplet as a picture dictionary. When discussing a topic requiring vocabulary at elementary/pre-intermediate level (housing, food, pets etc.), ask students to create their own picture dictionary using Popplet. They can do this in the computer lab or at home. Let students present their picture dictionaries on a projector or interactive whiteboard in class.

3.7 My thoughts 2.0

Application:	Voicethread, www.voicethread.com; lets your students collaboratively post their visual and oral associations with a certain topic.
Similar application:	Voxopop, www.voxopop.com
Focus:	collaborative brainstorming using text, image and speech
Level:	intermediate–advanced
Age:	mainly for over 13s; see Do It Yourself 1
Time:	45 minutes
ICT skills:	browsing, typing, copying & pasting, uploading, recording
Equipment:	computer lab OR single computer (headsets with microphone or laptop with built-in microphone recommended; if you cannot arrange microphones, you can still use Voicethread by using its written comment function); optional, projector

Do It Yourself

1 Register at www.voicethread.com. You must register in order to use the site. Any student under 13 must (a) use an account created by a parent or guardian and (b) have the explicit permission of their parent or guardian to use the service.

2 Click on 'Create' in the top left corner.

3 Then click on 'Upload from ... My Computer', choose an image and click on 'Open' to upload it (see Image 1).

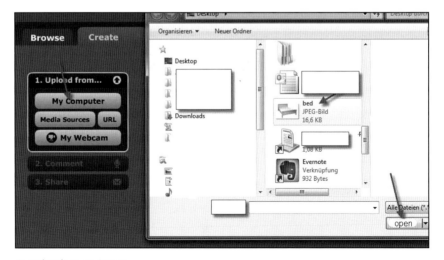

1: uploading an image

4   After the image has been uploaded, click on it, and then on 'Add a title and link' to take your image forwards, for example where the topic is dreams: 'Brainstorming sequence about dreams'.

5   Then click '2. comment' in the left control bar to record comments, either written or spoken.

6   In our example, we started by choosing a written comment (see Image 2) and we typed: 'Dear students! This is an interactive mindmapping/brainstorming application! Today's topic is 'dreams'. Please add all of the associations you have concerning the concept of 'dreams'. Enjoy!
    After you have typed in your comment, click 'Save'.

2: adding an instructional comment

7   Click on the 'play' button in order to see your comment (see Image 3).

3: watching the comments in context

8   Now your students are almost ready to start brainstorming the topic 'dreams'. In the control bar, click on '3. share'. Then click the 'Get a link' button, and see a small black box which allows you to adjust your privacy/collaboration settings. We recommend you tick 'allow anyone to view' and 'Comment'. (Don't worry! here, 'anyone' means just the people who will receive the URL from you.) Then click 'Copy the link' (see Image 4).

4: adjusting collaboration/privacy settings

9   Open a text document and paste the link into this to save it for the lesson; you may decide to project it or write it on the board for them.

in class

Lead-in

1   Depending on your students' age and level, put a controversial image on the board (e.g. someone smoking in a restaurant next to children).

2   Invite students to comment on this image orally and in words by writing their thoughts next to the image on the board.

3   Now tell your students that you are going to do the same procedure in a digitised way.

Online

1   Tell your students to register at www.voicethread.com, then sign in. Also show them how to upload a picture of themselves, as in Do It Yourself 3.

2   Tell them that today you are going to do visual and auditory brainstorming.

3   Project (or write) your Voicethread URL onto the board.

4   Students should type in the URL.

5   Now they can add as many comments (written/spoken) as they wish. Tell your students to write down/record anything and everything that comes into their minds on the topic of dreams.

Follow-up   In the next lesson, project the Voicethread onto the wall and play and pause it as needed in order to discuss the mindmapping process (give feedback, appreciate interesting associations, discuss mistakes etc.).

Variation 1 – Research map
For students at higher levels, you can use Voicethread for doing research on a particular topic. Upload an image about a topic and let them type/record information they have found out in books, on websites etc.

Variation 2 – Radio show
For students at higher levels, use Voicethread to produce a radio show. Let them create their own radio station logo. They can now use the 'record' function to broadcast a radio show on a chosen topic.

Variation 3 – 'I spy with my little eye'
For younger learners, use Voicethread to practise image descriptions. Upload a busy picture with a lot of things in it (e.g. an airport or a shopping arcade) and let the students record what they can see in the picture, using phrases like 'In this picture I can see a man writing in his notebook'.

Variation 4 – Comparisons
Upload a picture with two completely different objects/personalities etc. (e.g. Lady Gaga and The Beatles). Let students record their comparisons using appropriate grammatical structures, like 'Lady Gaga is crazier than the Beatles' etc.

3.7 My thoughts 2.0

Variation 5 – Fluency competition
For learners at higher levels, upload a picture for them to describe in as detailed a way as possible. The student with the longest and most fluent recorded description wins.

3.8 Another stick in the wall

Application:	Wallwisher, www.wallwisher.com; an online noticeboard maker which can be used for writing tasks and brainstorming sequences.
Similar application:	Pindax, www.pindax.com; Corkboard, www.corkboard.me
Focus:	collaborative mindmapping with sticky notes
Level:	pre-intermediate–advanced
Age:	any, so long as your students do not register
Time:	30 minutes
ICT skills:	browsing, typing, copying & pasting
Equipment:	computer lab OR single computer

Do It Yourself

1 Go to www.wallwisher.com. Click on 'Login' in the right top corner, then register.

   Note: you can also use Wallwisher without registering. However, you won't be able to save your mindmaps.

2 Click 'Build a wall' in the middle of the website.

3 Prepare basic settings. First type in the title and instructions for your mindmap, then choose an avatar image (see image 1).

1: basic settings

4 Then click on "Wallpaper" and choose a background (see image 2).

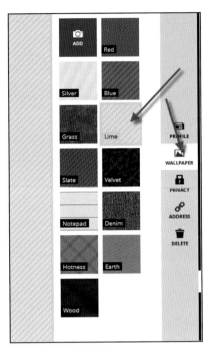

2: choosing a background

5   Then click on "Privacy" and choose your privacy settings (see image 3)

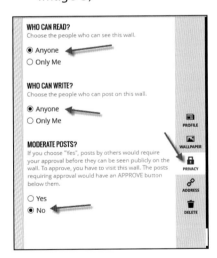

3: choosing your privacy settings

6   Click on "Address" and type in a URL for your students to click. Then click "OK" (see image 4).

3.8 Another stick in the wall

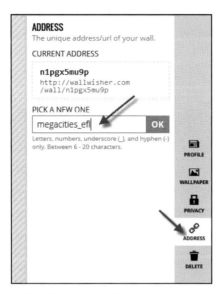

4: inserting a new address

7   Double-click anywhere in order to post your thoughts. You can also add an image with a link or a YouTube video (copy the URL from the YouTube video into the given field); in order to do that, click the little chain symbol. Then click 'OK' (see Image 5).

Note: You can drag the post to wherever you want and 'stick' it there. You can always edit your post by clicking the 'Edit' button.

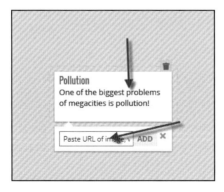

5: adding your thoughts

5   Copy the URL of your wall from the top browser bar.

Lead-in

1   Tell your students that they will have to reflect on the topic 'Problems of Megacities'.

2   Provide them with your URL.

Online

1   Now your students should post their thoughts on the topic.

   Note: They do not have to register; they can just type their names into a field when posting a thought.

2   After some time, discuss the posts by projecting the Wallwisher board onto the wall.

Variation 1 – 'Well, I must say ...'
You can use Wallwisher for feedback – after a lesson you have given, let students give feedback on your performance. Students can also post anonymously.

Variation 2 – 'Who am I ...?'
Use Wallwisher as a kind of quiz generator. Let students guess a certain person (celebrity, artist etc.) by posting a tiny hint every day (using words, videos, images etc.). If students know who you are posting about, they add a note with their guess (remembering to add their own names). The winner gets a prize.

Variation 3 – 'A word a day ...'
Use Wallwisher to post a new word, idiom, proverb etc. every day/ week etc. Students should try to find a translation and write a contextualised sentence using the word. You can give feedback by posting back.

Learn more
http://www.wallwisher.com/demo

3.9   I need a hand …

Application:	Tricider, www.tricider.com/en; lets you and your students create decision/opinion-making processes.
Similar application:	Polldaddy, www.polldaddy.com
Focus:	create simple decision-making processes
Level:	pre-intermediate–advanced
Age:	any
Time:	10–15 minutes
ICT skills:	browsing, typing
Equipment:	computer lab OR single computer.

Do It Yourself

1   Go to www.tricider.com/en. No registration is required.

2   Type in the problem/task. In this activity, you will be asking your students what they associate with a gap year. Then click 'Go' (see Image 1).

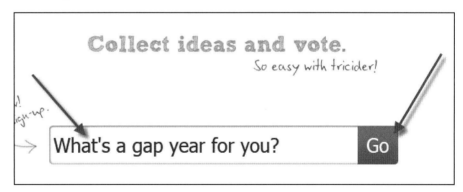

1: typing in the problem/task

3   Then click 'Add a description' and type in further instructions for your students (e.g. *Post two to three ideas in full sentences*), click 'Add idea' (see image 2) if you want to provide an example (e.g. 'Perfect possibility to relax'), then click 'Save'.

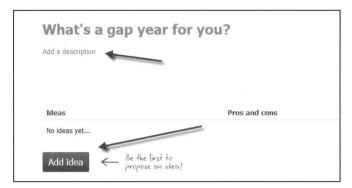

2: adding instructions

Then click 'share and invite'.

4   Then copy the link and keep it (see Image 3).

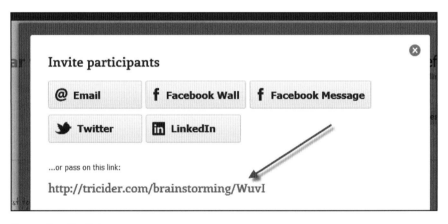

3: copying the link

in class

Lead-in

1   Tell your students that they are going to be asked about a certain topic and that they are invited to post their thoughts on it.

2   Give them your link.

Online

1   Now students should post several thoughts about the topic.

Top Tip 1: Your students will be able to add comments to their colleagues' opinions in the 'comments' field below.

Top Tip 2: Register for Tricider to save all of your 'Tricisions',

Variation – Tricider debate

Hold a debate on: death penalty; or living in the country vs living in a city; or living in a flat vs living in a house etc. First, students go and research their ideas plus some pros and cons. They could do this at home the day before, or be taken to the lab for 20 minutes. Then they report back to class (or stay in the lab). The tricider is projected and they have a whole class debate (or work in smaller groups) using the ideas displayed on the board.

CHAPTER 4
AUDIO

4.1 Do you speak ... Voki?

Application: Voki, www.voki.com (offers free premium account for teachers); lets students create their own avatar (i.e. their 'alter ego') on the internet, with personalised spoken messages.

Similar application: DoppelMe, www.doppelme.com

Focus: animated text/speech production using your avatar

Level: beginner–pre-intermediate

Age: any children under 13 using the site must be supervised and should not give any personal information. This means they cannot register – which means they cannot save or share their work – but they can still use the site to make a voki.

Time: 60 minutes

ICT skills: browsing, basic navigation skills, uploading

Equipment: computer lab or stand-alone computer; microphone; a device to time 1 and 2 minutes

Preparation: In a run-up lesson, help your age 13+ students register for Voki; tell them to open www.voki.com. Show them how the registration process works; depending on the level of your students, you can explain everything in English, so they get acquainted with IT-specific vocabulary (*log on, register, browser* etc.).
An activation link (with all the login data) will be sent to the students' email addresses. Now your students will be able to log on to Voki.

Do It Yourself

1   Go to www.voki.com and click 'Register' (see Image 1).

1: registration process

2   Fill in the application form (see Image 2).

2: filling in the application form

3   When the registration process is complete, in www.voki.com click 'Create' (see Image 3). Move your mouse around the page and watch what happens!

3: creating a Voki

4   Now you can choose from a variety of characters. You can adapt certain features like type of avatar, hair colour etc. (see Image 4). When you have finished, click 'Done' (see Image 5).

4: customising your character

5: done

5   Then you can make your avatar speak by clicking one of the Give
    it a Voice options. You can record by phone, type in a text (that
    becomes speech), record your own audio (with a microphone) or
    upload an audio file (see Image 6).

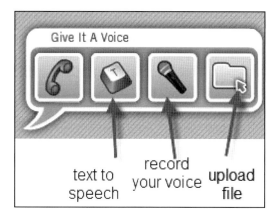

6: making your avatar speak

6   Our example below shows how to introduce yourself with Voki. Click on 'Text to speech' and write a short introduction. You can choose the variety of English and the voice (male/female) of various speakers (see Image 7). After typing in the text, you can listen to your Voki by clicking on the 'Play' button beneath the picture. When you are satisfied, click 'Done'.

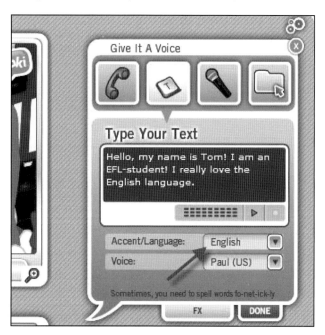

7: writing a text (short introduction)

7   Click on 'Backgrounds' (see Image 8) to select your choice, then 'Done.

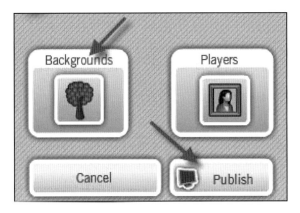

8: adjusting background and publishing

8   As you have registered, you can publish your Voki (see Image 8 again). Click 'Publish' and follow through. At the end, click the black arrow at 'Or, get your Voki link here' and choose 'Standard Voki link'. Then copy the URL.

in class

Lead-in

1   Tell your students to relax and lean back.

2   Then tell them to close their eyes. When you say 'Go', they should think of some basic information they would provide to a new classmate; e.g. if you are covering 'leisure time' in your lessons, tell your students to think about the leisure-time activities they do. Tell them you'll give them 1 minute to silently think about this topic. After the minute say: 'Stop!' Tell your students to open their eyes again.

3   Now tell your students to take a sheet of paper and tell them that when you say 'Go!' they will get 2 minutes to write brief notes on the information they were thinking about. Once you've started them off, give them 2 minutes and then say: 'Stop!'

4   Ask some students to present their results to the class.

Online

1   Tell your students to log on to Voki with their account.

2   Then they click on the 'Create' button, create their character, and choose its features.

3   They then can make their avatar speak by clicking one of the Give it a Voice options. We suggest you tell students to introduce themselves by clicking on 'Text to speech' and writing a short introduction (including some of their leisure time associations from the 'Lead-in' task).

4   Just as you did, they can choose the variety of English and the voice (male/female) of various speakers, then they can listen to their Voki by clicking on the 'Play' button beneath the picture. When they are satisfied, they click 'Done'.

5   They can adjust the background and those who have registered can publish their Voki. Under 13s will be able to look at each other's vokis on the different computers.

Variation 1 – Other ideas for Vokis

By creating Vokis, students produce short texts within a highly creative context. As well as a short introduction of themselves, topics for them to present could include:

- hobbies
- family
- my hometown
- favourite music
- my favourite animal
- at the weekend

Variation 2 – My Voki speaking

You can tell students at any level to record their own voices (see Image 6) by using a microphone. You can use topics from the list above.

Variation 3 – Reading a passage in my own voice

Let your students read a passage from a newspaper article or from a novel (they should record it on Voki). They should adapt the outer appearance of their Voki and voice to the text type (e.g. newspaper article: serious reporter, standard English).

Variation 4 – Reading a passage in another voice

You can do the same activity as in Variation 2, but this time let students type in a certain passage (or even copy and paste a passage and edit it) and let them choose the native speaker included in Voki (e.g. Allison – American English, Alan – Australian English, Audrey – British English).

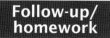
Follow-up/ homework

1   For homework, tell your students to think about a famous person/ celebrity.

2   Tell them to create a Voki which resembles the character in some way. Then they should type or record a text that describes the personality quite well without mentioning the name; e.g. I live in LA. I am an actor. My favourite genre is action. I was governor of California. (*Arnold Schwarzenegger*).

Do you speak ... Voki?

3   In class, your students present their famous Vokis. The others guess who it is.

More ideas
http://www.voki.com/lesson_plans.php

4.2   'Listen up! That's me!'

Application:	Audioboo, www.audioboo.fm; a web platform that allows students and teachers to record their audio files and share them with their friends, classmates etc.
Similar application:	www.ipadio.com, www.vocaroo.com
Focus:	create audio files of spoken interaction/podcasts
Level:	elementary
Age:	13+ only; under-18s who use the site should have their parent's or guardian's permission to do so
Time:	60 minutes
ICT skills:	browsing, basic navigation skills, tagging, audio recording
Equipment:	computer lab OR single computer, headsets (earphones + microphone)

Do It Yourself

1   Go to www.audioboo.fm and sign up.

2   Then click on 'Make a Recording/Upload File' (see Image 1).

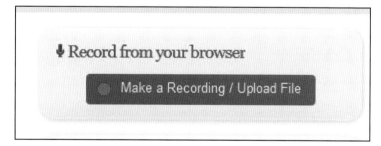

1: to record an audio file

3   Now record a presentation. To do this, click 'Got your mic ready?' then click through the security information system to get to 'Start Recording'. After you have finished recording, click on 'Pause Recording'.

4   Then click on 'Happy? Add a title' and add a title to your recording (see Image 2). You can also add tags, i.e. words that are associated with this recording in order to find the archived recording more quickly. And you can add a picture of yourself by clicking 'Image' (see Image 2). After that, click 'Publish' (see Image 2 again) and wait for a few minutes. Then click 'here' when you read 'Awesome, thanks for the boo. After a bit of processing you'll be able to find it here.'

4.2 'Listen up! That's me!'

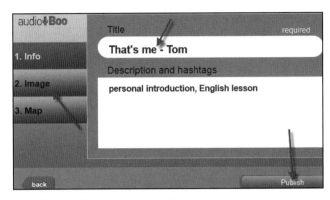

2: adding a title to your recording

5 Now you have created your first Audioboo recording. You can listen to it by clicking on the Play button (see Image 3) – or, if you've been away from the page or site, you can find your recording under 'My Profile'. To share this audio file, paste the link into the URL bar and email it to whoever you want. You and your students will be able to listen to the recording and add constructive feedback by writing comments or recording audio feedback (see Image 4).

3: listening to your audio file

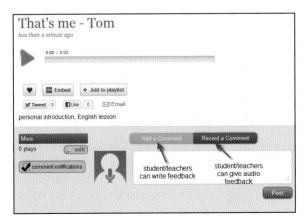

4: giving feedback

6 Tell your students to go to www.audioboo.fm and show them how the signup process works. Depending on the level of your students, you can explain everything in English so they get acquainted with IT-specific vocabulary (*log on*, *register*, *browser* etc.).

in class

Lead-in

1 Tell your students that in the next activity it is very important that they speak clearly.

2 Tell them that they should write a short text about themselves (e.g. a short introduction: name, age, home, hobbies etc., about 70 words) to be read later on.

3 Give your students 10 minutes to write and practise their texts.

4 Tell your students to think of a 'concept' of how to put their text into an audio presentation. The following ideas might help: name, age, home, hobbies, favourite pets, favourite actors/actresses, favourite sportsmen, favourite meal etc. Their presentation should be short, not longer than two minutes (though Audioboo will allow you to record three-minute audio chunks).

5 Students should practise their presentations with their partners.

Online

1 Tell them to log on to Audioboo with their account, then click on 'Make a Recording/Upload File'. Remind them that it will be important for them to speak clearly.

2 Now let your students record their presentations, and when they have finished recording, click on 'Pause Recording' then add a title.

3 Tell your students to make the title a catchy one. They can also add tags and a picture of themselves. After that, they click 'Publish'.

4 Now your students have created their first audio recording. They can listen to it by clicking on the play button, or if they've gone away from the page or site, they can find their recordings under 'My Profile'.

5 If your students want to share this audio file, they paste the link into the URL bar and send it to the people they want (e.g. you!). You and your students can listen to the recording and add constructive feedback by writing comments or recording audio feedback.

4.2 'Listen up! That's me!'

Variation 1 – 'Tell me what you think'

With higher-level students, you could pre-record a controversial question, then ask the students to present their opinion by recording a boo (Audioboo sound file). You will need to record a boo on the topic (e.g. 'Would you ban smoking in public places?'), provide the link to the audio file and let students express their opinions by adding an audio comment (see Image 4). The great advantage is that students can also listen to other students' opinions.

Variation 2 – 'Please carry on …'

With intermediate –advanced students, you can produce an audio story. Pre-record a boo by starting with a story (e.g. *Once upon a time there was a rich man in New York who loved expensive clothes* …), and provide the link to the students. Also, in your boo, give instructions telling the students to continue the story with 2–3 sentences by recording a boo of their own. After one student has posted a continuation to the beginning of the story, another student can carry on narrating the story.

Top Tip: before you let your students record their boos, decide on a sequence (who starts, who comes next etc.)

Variation 3 – Dream job – narrator

In order to make students aware of the importance of reading and the nature of language (intonation, pronunciation, stress etc.), let them read a short piece of a text (short story, poem, tongue twister). They record their reading and share it with their classmates or you, who can then give feedback.

Variation 4 – Book report – the spoken way

With higher-level students, you can carry out a book report via Audioboo. After students have read a certain book, ask them to provide a short audio summary or to present book-related tasks via a recording. Again, their classmates and/or you can come up with feedback.

Follow-up/ homework

1   For homework, tell your students to edit their own audio file (i.e. listen over and over again for mistakes, mispronounced words etc. in order to re-record a corrected version).

2   Tell your students to send the link of their audio files to you, so that you can give them audio feedback on their new recordings.

More ideas
http://audioboo.fm/about/audioboo

4.3 'Voice upon a time ...'

Application:	Little Bird Tales, www.littlebirdtales.com; lets your students create audio tales with text and pictures.
Similar application:	Toondoo, www.toondoo.com (see Activity 5.6)
Focus:	creating audio tales with text and pictures
Level:	pre-intermediate–intermediate
Age:	best for children aged 3–14
Time:	60–120 minutes
ICT skills:	browsing, typing, recording, uploading
Equipment:	computer lab OR single computer, smartphones or dictaphones owned by students; USB sticks owned by students; headset (inc. microphone); speakers compatible with students' smartphones (for the lead-in).

Preparation:

1 In a run-up lesson, tell your students to write a fairy tale on a computer. You can suggest various things to be included depending on level (characters, content words, linking words, setting etc.). Tell them too that this kind of story always includes an adversity to be overcome (for lots more about this, see Helbling Language's *Writing Stories*). Also, make sure your students try to find digital pictures associated with the story; for each paragraph they should find at least one picture (in a jpeg, gif or png file). If the students have completed PiratePad, Activity 3.1, they could use the story they generated there.
Tell your students to bring the text along in digital form (on a USB stick/flash drive/pen drive) for the lesson.

2 Tell the students who have dictaphones or smartphones that they should pick one of their favourite fairy tales and read them (or at least some passages) at home while recording themselves, and bring the recording into class for the lesson, as well.

Do It Yourself

1 Create an account at www.littlebirdtales.com. You will need to sign in as a teacher and register your school name, and you will be given a school code.

2 Click 'Create a Tale'. The computer asks you to grant access for Flash Player to your computer; click 'Allow'. Now type in the title of your tale, and your name, and click 'Save and Continue'. You can also upload a picture for the cover (see Image 1).

1: creating a tale

3   To record a story: write a text in the 'Add Text:' box, and click the round green button (see Image 2) and speak, starting with your tale.

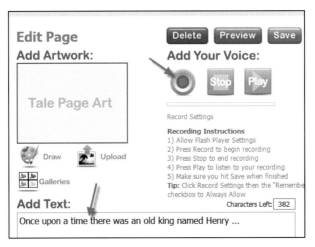

2: starting the recording

4   When you have finished, click 'Stop'. You can listen to your recording by clicking 'Play'. If you don't like it, you can click the green button again to re-record.

5   You can upload a picture (see Image 3) to match the title, text or recorded audio. The image must be a jpeg, gif or png file. Then click 'Save' (see Image 3).

3: basic settings (uploading pictures etc.)

6   Now you can add as many pages as you want for your story. You can record paragraph by paragraph, can also add some text in the 'Add text' field and can add more pictures.

7   When you have finished, click 'Save' and then 'Preview' (see Images 4 and 5).

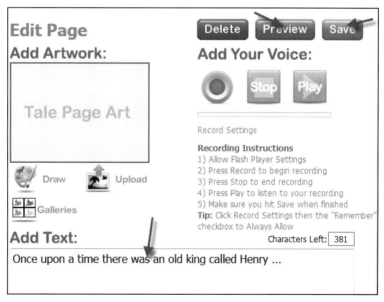

4: Save and Preview

5: preview of audio tale

8   In Preview mode, click on the 'Embed Code' button at the bottom, and copy the URL link to share your story with your students.

Lead-in

1   In class, let some students present their podcasts (using speakers plugged into their smartphone or dictaphone).

2   Tell your students that they will be adding audio and pictures to the fairy tales they have written and brought in with them.

Online

1   Help your students register at www.littlebirdtales.com, signing in with your school code.

2   Explain to your students how Little Bird Tales works. To get started, they click 'Create a Tale' then 'Allow' Flash Player.

3   The first thing the students should do is type in the title of their tale and their name, then click 'Save and Continue'.

4   Now it is time for the students to start recording their tale. Tell them to speak fairly quietly since they are in the computer lab with other students.

5   To record a voice, they click in the 'Add Text:' box, then click the round green button and speak. When they have finished the first paragraph, they click 'Stop', then listen to their recording by

clicking 'Play'. If they don't like it the first time (which will almost certainly be the case), they can click the green button again to re-record.

6   They can upload a picture to match the title (if it doesn't work, remind them that it must be a jpeg, gif or png file). Then they click 'Save and Continue'.

7   Now your students can add as many pages they want for their story. They can record paragraph by paragraph, can also add some text in the 'Add text' field and can add more pictures.

8   When they have finished, students click 'Save' and then 'Preview'.

9   In Preview mode, students can also copy the URL to share their efforts with you and their classmates.

Variation – Various text types
Your students can also use Little Bird Tales for creating different text types. Provide a controversial picture, tell students to upload this picture to Little Bird Tales and let them comment on it. You can also let your students produce book reports by using the cover of a book for your students to provide an oral book review.

Follow-up/ homework

1   Tell your students to share their stories with their classmates. Each story needs to be given feedback by a classmate. The feedback can be given orally in the next lesson or in written form as homework. The 'feedbacker' should give the producer oral or written feedback taking the following things into account:
   • Task achieved? (Is it really a fairy tale?)
   • Coherence/cohesion (Is the text fluent and easy to read?)
   • Grammar (What about grammar? Any mistakes? Solid use of grammar?)
   • Vocabulary (What about vocabulary? Any mistakes? Use of idioms, good phrases etc.)
   • Creativity/layout (What about the creativity of the plot? What about layout? Good use of pictures? Consistent layout?)
   • Content (Did you like the story? Which was your favourite part?)

   Note: It is important to tell your students that they should focus on the positive aspects of the text!

2   In addition to feeding back, the student writes a sequel to the fairy tale he/she gave feedback on.

Variation 1 – A certain passage ...
Ask students to pick a certain scene/passage from their fairy tale. Tell them to write a dialogue between the protagonists from this scene.

Variation 2 – Diary entry

Tell your student to pick one character from their story. They should write a diary entry pretending to be this person.

Learn more

http://littlebirdtales.com/tales/default/

4.4 'This is school radio!'

Application: Spreaker, www.spreaker.com; lets your students easily create dynamic radio shows.

Focus: producing radio shows/podcasts

Level: intermediate–advanced.

Age: preferably 18+; must definitely be 13+

Time: 120 minutes

ICT skills: browsing, typing, uploading, recording

Equipment: computer lab OR single computer, microphone OR computer with built-in microphone; the computer(s) you use will need to be accessed by Adobe Flash Player; a device to time 30 seconds

Preparation:

1 Before the lesson, you might like to give your students some preparation of their own, to be done either at home or in a previous lesson.
Give them a celebrity name and a worksheet with some bullet points:
   - Real name
   - Date of birth
   - Place of birth
   - Profession
   - Hobbies
   - Dark secrets
   - Biggest achievements/successes

   To find answers to these, they would need to look for information online (Wikipedia, a YouTube interview, the celebrity Facebook account or their own site).
   Using the information they have gathered, they should prepare a set of questions and answers (encourage them to just make notes, not write a full script to read out), and then, using their notes, they can make the recordings using their smartphones.

2 Draft a script for your radio show. Here are some stock phrases; you can incorporate some of them into your show, and reproduce the list as a handout for students.

   Introduction
   - Hello dear listeners, and welcome to today's edition of 'Susi's Movie Stars'!
   - Welcome everybody to my lovely show, 'Susi's Movie Stars'!
   - Hey folks! What's up? Welcome to my show, 'Susi's Movie Stars'!

Main part
- Let's talk about a cool film called 'Bee Movie'.
- In today's show, we're gonna rate 'Ocean's Twelve'.
- Today our experts will rate 'The Devil wears Prada'.

Conclusion
- That was it for today's show. Hope you enjoyed it. See you next week! Same time, same place! My name is Will Turner for Radio Heustadelgasse.
- Keep it real! Bye!

Do It Yourself

1   Register ('Create a free account') at www.spreaker.com ('signup without using Facebook'). **Note:** You can change the language at the bottom of the webpage.

2   Click on 'Broadcast' and type into the fields. Then click 'Next' (see Image 1).

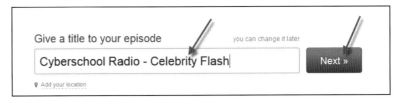

1: providing relevant information

3   Now you can record your radio show. Click on 'record a new podcast', then the red record button, then speak (see Image 2). After your recording, click on the record button again.

2: recording radio show

4   Now you can listen to your recording by clicking 'Play' on the pre-player (see Image 3). When you are satisfied, click 'Close' in the top right corner.

3: listening to the recording

5   If you want to add sound effects or your own audio files, click on the '+' next to 'Sound fx' in the right bottom corner, choose an effect, then click '+ add' and/or 'Upload' in the left top corner (see Image 4). Then click 'Close' in the top right corner. You can play your sound effects anytime you want to, including during the recording, just like in a real radio studio.

4: adding sound effects or audio files

6   When you are finished with your radio show, click the 'Publish' button, then 'Yes, publish' (see Image 5).

5: publishing the radio show

7   Click on 'Edit' to add details. Then click 'Save', then 'Next'.

8   Now click on 'Your episodes' (on top in the middle). Click on your recorded episode, then 'Share'. Now copy the URL (see Image 6).

6: getting the radio show URL

Top Tip: Top Tip: If you click the black arrow pointing downwards, you can also download your show (see Image 7)

7: downloading your show

Lead-in

1   Ask your students to get a blank sheet of paper, then tell them that they are going to produce a radio show.

2   Tell them that they should not write their name on the paper. They will have 30 seconds to write down everything that comes to mind when thinking of the following statement: 'A good radio show needs …'. After 30 seconds, tell the students to stop writing and to pass the sheet to their neighbour.

3   Now for another 30 seconds, students should add their comments to the sheet of paper they have received. Repeat this procedure 2–3 times.

4   Then let students read out the comments on the sheets. Discuss in class.

5   Hand out your phrases, then on a mindmap on the board, ask students to come up with typical radio show phrases.

Online

1   Tell your students that they will produce a radio show about their favourite celebrity.

2   Present your example of a radio show.

3   Show your students how Spreaker works.

4   Give them plenty of time to try things out, and to work on their radio show. Tell them that one person is the radio show host and that the other person is the celebrity. They should carry out an interview. Tell them to include sound effects, songs etc. as in Do It Yourself Step 5.

5   When your students have finished, tell them to copy the URL of their radio show.

Follow-up

1   In the next lesson they should present their radio shows; give them plenty of time to present/play their interviews.

2   For homework, ask your students to interview their parents, friends etc. about their favourite celebrities. Students can use Spreaker, but also an mp3 recorder, their smartphones or a sheet of paper to record/write down the interview.

Note: If they are going to record their interviews on their smartphones, tell them that they should save them on a pen/ flash drive/USB stick, or email you the files, so you can prepare to present the files in class.

Learn more
http://www.spreaker.com/page#!/cms/tutorial

CHAPTER 5
WRITING

5.1 My online book project

Application:	Livebinders, www.livebinders.com; allows its users to organise their resources in an online binder.
Similar application:	Penzu, www.penzu.com. Note: there is also Penzu Classroom for teachers. www.penzu.com/classroom
Focus:	students present their creative outcomes online
Level:	pre-intermediate–advanced
Age:	any, but see Do It Yourself 1
Time:	school year
ICT skills:	uploading, browsing, structuring
Equipment:	computer lab OR single computer

Do It Yourself

1   Sign yourself up for Livebinders. NB students under 13 may not enter their own email addresses but must use a teacher-generated (gmail) address. The Livebinders site makes this procedure very simple, but you will need to ensure that you have a suitable (gmail) address.

2   Click 'Start a Blank Binder' (left hand side) and type in the required fields. In the example is a Livebinder for a book project on 'About a Boy' (see Image 1).

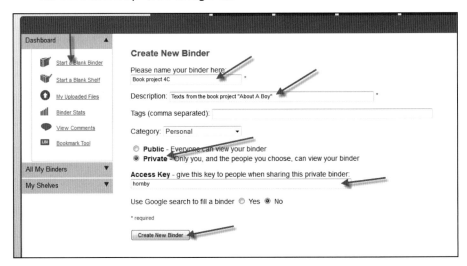

1: basic settings

Note: Select the option 'Private' to choose the people who can view your binder.

3   Then click 'Edit Menu' in the right top corner once or twice. A menu will open where you can upload your assignments for the book project (click 'Upload File'), in our example a fictional interview with the protagonist (see Image 2).

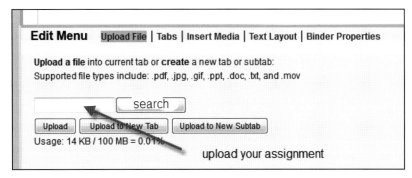

2: uploading assignment

4   Then you will need to add titles to your binder tabs (see Image 3). You can do this by navigating to the main page (click on the Livebinders logo on the top left); then click 'All my binders', then 'My private binders'. Choose your binder and click 'edit'. and click on the title of your binder.

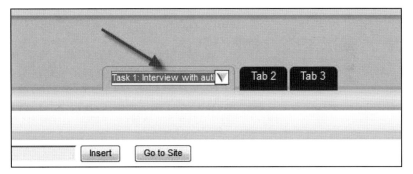

3: add titles to your tabs

5   You can also add a link to a webpage (see Image 4).

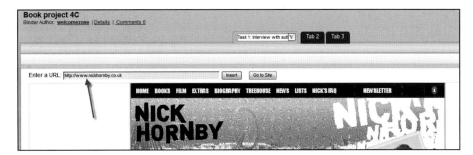

4: adding links

6   You can add as many forms of media as you like (documents, photos, videos etc.) In order to do so, click 'Edit Menu' once or twice (top right corner).

Lead-in

1   Tell your students that they are going to do an online book project running throughout the school year using Livebinders (tell them that you will show them later how to use the program).

2   Explain the tasks to your students; here are some ideas that are suitable for a book project:

a. Reading log/diary
   - Write a reading log/diary. Every time you read part of your book, write a diary entry about it. The following aspects must be included in each entry:
     o date
     o number of pages you've read
     o mini-summary of what you've read (2-4 sentences)
     o what you liked best
     o what you didn't really like
     o your personal thoughts (protagonists' actions, what will happen next etc.).
   - Try to design your reading log/diary in a neat way (using colours, pictures etc.).

b. Presentation
   - Prepare a 15-minute presentation about a book. (Remember to state the date you'll do the presentation!)
   - Your presentation should include: *plot, *characters, *quotations, *personal opinion, *pictures etc.

c. Design a fan website
   - Design a fan website about the book, including protagonist, author etc. (not real ones, of course ☺)
   - Visit some other fan websites (e.g. beatlefans.com or http://www.startrek.com/fan_sites) to get your ideas!
   - Think of a coherent structure for your site.
   - Then summarise the plot in your OWN words.

d. You are an author
   - Imagine you are a famous author and your publishing house has asked you to write another book/novel/short story.
   - Write a similar story based on a book you've read (about 300-500 words).

e. Writing to/about an author
   - Write a letter/email to an author. Tell them what you like about their work and the novel, what you find good/bad, or what you do not understand. You may ask them questions.

- Create a digital poster/ad with a picture of an author, list of other works (titles) and a few lines on their book.

f. Plot
  - Write a review of the book.
  - Make a timeline of the events in the story, and explain it.
  - Summarise the plot by creating a cartoon version of the novel. Use about 6–8 frames. You can use www.goanimate.com or www.toondoo.com (see Activity 5.6).

g. Themes
  - Find ten keywords/phrases and explain their meaning (e.g. Harry Potter – magic).
  - Choose five quotations from the book and explain why you like them.
  - Put together a collage of the main ideas/themes of the story.

h. Language and setting:
  - Write a different ending for the novel.

3   Here are some more tasks (source: www.teachnet.com):

- Task 1 – Interview
  Interview a character from your book. Write at least ten questions that will give the character the opportunity to discuss his/her thoughts and feelings about his/her role in the story. The way you choose to present your interview is up to you.
- Task 2 – Diary
  Write a diary that one of the story's main characters might have kept before, during or after the book's events. Remember that the character's thoughts and feelings are very important in a diary.
- Task 3 – Sales talk
  Draft a sales talk, pretending you are a clerk in a bookstore and you want to push this book.
- Task 4 – Writing a movie script
  Imagine that you are the author of the book you have just read. Suddenly the book becomes a best seller. Write a letter to a movie producer trying to get that person interested in making your book into a movie. Explain why the story, characters, conflicts etc., would make a good film. Suggest a film location and actors to play the various roles. **You may only use books which have not already been made into movies.**
- Task 5 – Review
  Write a book review as it would be done for a newspaper. (Be sure you read a few before writing your own.)

- Task 6 – Letter
  Write a letter (10-sentence minimum) to the main character of your book, asking questions, protesting about a situation, and/or making a complaint and/or a suggestion. This must be done in the correct letter format.
- Task 7 – Live reporter
  Be a TV or radio reporter, and draft a report of a scene from the book as if it is happening 'live'.
- Task 8 – The message
  Write about what you have learnt from the story (about 100 words).
- Task 9 – Travel brochure
  Create a travel brochure promoting the place that is the setting for the story.

Online

1   In the computer lab, show your students how to sign up for Livebinders, using either their own email address or, if they are under 13, the gmail address you have generated.

2   Tell your students that they will need Livebinders for the presentation of their book project, i.e. they will be allowed to present the tasks online in their personal learning journal.

3   Tell your students to click 'Start a Blank Binder' and type into the fields.

4   Then they should click 'Edit Menu' in the right top corner so that they can upload their assignments for the book project.

5   Show your students how to add titles to their binder tabs and how to add various media such as webpages, documents, photos, videos etc.).

6   Tell them they can use Livebinders for a book project. When the deadline falls due, students can send their Livebinder URL (including keyword) to you.

To do this, they click on 'All my binders' (in the main menu), then on 'Private Binders', then on the 'Book Project' binder, click on 'Present' (and then copy) and then copy your URL from the browser (see Images 5 and 6).

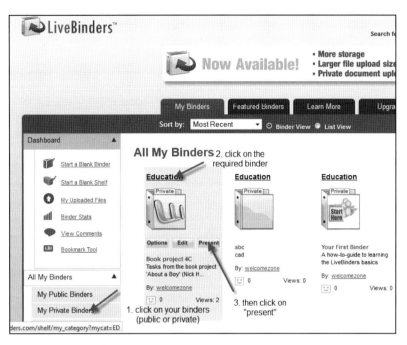

5: finding the teacher's URL, stage 1

6: finding the teacher's URL, stage 2

Variation 1 – I wanna share it with my mates

In order to support collaborative working, tell your students that they can also use Livebinders to share learning material (glossaries, useful grammar handouts, good summaries etc.) with each other.

Variation 2 – EFL teacher corner

Show Livebinders to your teacher colleagues; by using it, you can easily share useful information. You could even create a school Livebinder for EFL teachers to share links, videos, handouts etc.

When all students have finished their online projects, collect their Livebinder links and make these accessible to the other students using a 'backchannelling' app like Todaysmeet (see Activity 3.4).

Follow-up

Learn more
http://www.livebinders.com/?type=video

5.2

My flipbook story

Application:	Flipsnack, www.flipsnack.com; allows students to create their own flipbooks.
Similar application:	Issuu, www.issuu.com; Youblisher, www.youblisher.com
Focus:	embed written texts into flipbooks
Level:	elementary–pre-intermediate
Age:	13+ only; also, any student under the age of consent in the country where they are located must have the permission of parent/guardian to use the website
Time:	50 minutes
ICT skills:	creating pdf files, uploading, browsing
Equipment:	text processing software (e.g. Word), pen drive; computer lab OR single computer

Preparation:

1 Check the computers you plan to use in the lesson to ensure you know how they will make pdfs from text documents.

2 In a run-up lesson, tell your students to write an adventure story using font size 12 or 14 pt, line spacing one-and-a-half or double, and two pages minimum. The choice of story content and characters is up to you and the class between you. You might like to tell them that creating a story means thinking of a difficulty and an interesting way of overcoming it. (For lots more information about helping students write stories, see another title in Helbling Language's Resourceful Teacher series: *Writing Stories.*)

3 Tell your students to save their story on a pen drive/flash drive/ USB stick which they should bring along for the lesson.

Do It Yourself

1 Go to www.flipsnack.com and register; you can do this with your email account, or with a Facebook or Twitter or Google account.

2 Open a text file and convert it into a pdf. Sometimes you can print your document to pdf, in others you may need to click on File, then either Export or Save As > File type: pdf (see Image 1). More information is on our website. If all else fails, in a search engine type in ".doc to .pdf converter" (or instead of .doc, enter .docx or .odt or other file type). Save the new pdf file.

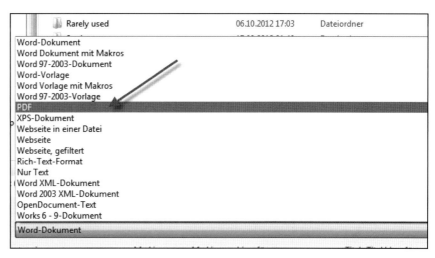

1: converting your file into a pdf. NB This example is based on Word 2010.

3   When you have created your pdf, open Flipsnack and click 'Make a flipping book'.

4   Give your story a title and upload your pdf file (see Image 2). Wait until your file is uploaded. Then click 'Next'.

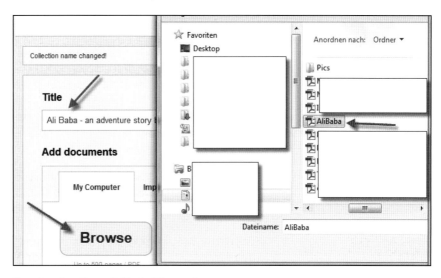

2: uploading the pdf file to Flipsnack

5   The next step is to choose a flipbook template (see Image 3); you can choose colours, sizes etc. Then scroll down and click 'Finish'.

5.2 My flipbook story

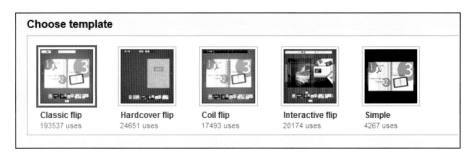

3: choosing a template

6   Now you have turned your text into a highly visual flipbook (see image 4).

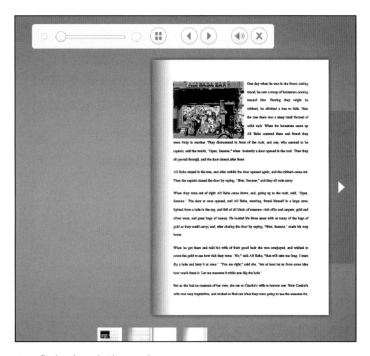

4: a flipbook with Flipsnack

7   Copy the link below, or click on one of the sharing options available.

Lead-in

1   Get the students into groups of 3–5 to share their stories.

2   Then each group chooses a story and they mime it to the class.

Online

1   In the computer lab, show your students your flipbook, and tell them that Flipsnack is an application that allows them to put their written texts into a highly creative flipbook.

2   Now each student should open the file with their adventure story. If your students don't know how to add pictures to their texts, now is the time to tell them.

3   Next, they need to convert their Word file into a pdf. If they don't know how to do it on the computer they're using, show them.

4   After students have created their pdfs, tell them to go to www.flipsnack.com. Show them how to register and log in.

5   They click 'Make a flipping book', give their story a title and upload their pdf file. Then they click 'Next', and choose a flipbook template, then click 'Finish'.

6   When the link appears, students can send their story to you to read.

Variation 1 – Tourist brochure
Your students can also create a tourist brochure with Flipsnack. When your students are doing cultural studies, Flipsnack is a powerful tool to create travel brochures on New York, London, Australia etc.

Variation 2 – Book project
Students can also use Flipsnack in order to present a book project.

Variation 3 – Class newspaper
Use Flipsnack to create a class newspaper.

Follow-up/ homework

1   For homework, tell your students to give their flipbook link to a colleague, who should give constructive feedback on the story (feedback can be typed into Flipsnack). Here are some ideas the feedback could focus on:

- Task achievement (Is it really an adventure story?)
- Coherence/cohesion (Is the text fluent and easy to read?)
- Grammar (What about grammar? Any mistakes? Solid use of grammar?)
- Vocabulary (What about vocabulary? Any mistakes? Use of idioms, good phrases etc.)
- Creativity/layout (What about the creativity of the plot? What about layout? Good use of pictures? Consistent layout?)

Note: It is important to tell your students that they should focus on the positive aspects of the text!

Learn more
http://www.flipsnack.com/flip-book-template/

5.3

Things I learnt today

Application: Penzu, www.penzu.com; allows you and your students to keep personal diaries online. Penzu offers a very appealing surface for students.

Similar application: Livebinders, www.livebinders.com (see Activity 5.1)

Focus: create your personal online diary

Level: upper intermediate–advanced

Age: 13+ only; it is requested that students aged 13-18 years ask their parent/guardian for permission to use the site

Time: 10 minutes

ICT skills: browsing, uploading

Equipment: computer lab OR single computer

Do It Yourself

1   Sign up at Penzu and create a journal.

2   Click on your journal icon (see Image 1).

1: opening a new entry

3   Now you can write about anything you like, using Penzu. This application is very simple to handle (including its settings, see Image 2).

5.3 Things I learnt today

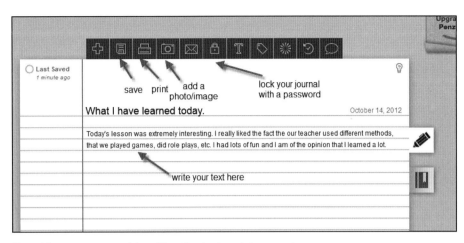

2: writing an entry and handling the text and document

in class

Lead-in

1 Drawing a mindmap on the board, ask your students about the things that can be learnt in an EFL lesson. Possible answers might be:
   - grammar
   - new words/vocabulary
   - cultural studies.

2 When eliciting certain aspects of things to learn in an EFL classroom, always let your students explain WHY certain things are that important and how they would need them in real life.

Online

1 Show your students how to register for Penzu and create their own journal.

2 Then tell your students to put their computers or put them on standby (unless you're using them for another activity). Continue with your regular lesson.

3 15 minutes before the end of the lesson, invite your students to write an online journal entry about what they have learnt today, what they liked about the lesson and what they did not really like. They should click on their journal icon and write about what they have learnt in today's lesson, using Penzu.

Note: The computer lab is not, of course, the same as the classroom setting (which probably has no computers), but once the students know how to work with Penzu they will be able to give you feedback about your regular lessons on their own computers.

Variation 1 – Personal portfolio

Your students can use Penzu as a personal portfolio for their book projects, learning journals etc.

Variation 2 – Writing, writing, writing

Penzu can be used in order to practise various text types in your EFL lessons. Students can focus on the actual writing process in a graphically appealing online diary.

Follow-up

1   Invite your students to use Penzu as often as possible – at least four times a school year and preferably more. This is a great activity to keep track of things learnt and to see one's own progress in learning a language.

2   During the school year from time to time, ask your students to read from their Penzu journals (on a voluntary basis). This is a great way for you to learn about your lessons/teaching style.

Can you see? – it's 3D!

Application:	Zooburst, www.zooburst.com, lets your students create 3D-flipbooks, ideal for story-telling.
Similar application:	Storybird, www.storybird.com (see Activity 2.7)
Focus:	creating 3D flipbook stories
Level:	beginner–intermediate.
Age:	over 13 years, though if you have an Educator account (see Do It Yourself 1), students can be any age
Time:	60 minutes
ICT skills:	browsing, typing, copying & pasting, uploading
Equipment:	computer lab OR single computer, USB stick/pen drive/flash drive
Preparation:	If you want your students to prepare their own pictures for a particular kind of story, tell them the lesson before, to give them a chance to research these online in their own time.

Do It Yourself

1   Register at www.zooburst.com. You need to register in order to use the program. You may choose to register as an Educator, with a paid subcription providing features including a classroom management tool. Or you can have a Basic account, which is free.

2   In order to work with Zooburst in class, you will need to create a 3D-flipbook yourself.

3   Click on 'My books' in the top control bar, then 'New book'.

4   Then type into the required fields (for 'who can see this book', pick 'Only people with a valid password' and click 'Save' (see Image 1).

5.4 Can you see? – it's 3D!

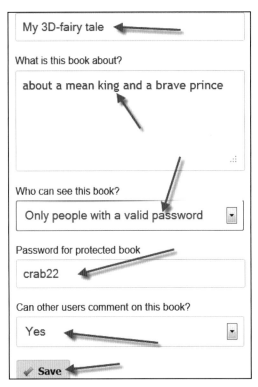

1: providing main information

5   To find images for your story, you can use the built-in clipart search engine. To do this, in the left-hand 'Pictures' panel, type a keyword into the text box and key Return or click on the magifying glass icon. Or, you click on the binoculars icon beneath the text entry field; then in the centre panel, headed 'Browse Clip Art Library', select a letter from the dropdown list, then a keyword. Either way, watch the image(s) appear in the left-hand panel. When you have found an image you want, click on it so that it appears in the flipbook. This first page will be the cover of your book, so in the 'Page narration' field, type a title, and when you're done, click on the green tick at top right.

You can also use your own images from your PC or USB stick; to do this, click the green up-arrow on the left (see Image 2), then browse to select the picture you want.

If you have an interactive whiteboard or a computer and a projector, look for pictures of words you'll use in Lead-in Step 1, and copy and paste them into a digital document.

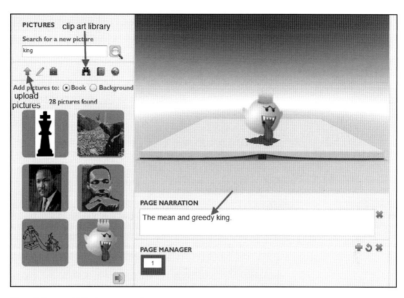

2: adding a title to your story

6   Add a new page by clicking on the green plus sign in the bottom right corner (see Image 2 again). Then add the images/characters you want. Again, write something in the 'page narration' field.

7   You can let your characters 'speak' by clicking on them and adding the text they are supposed to say (see Image 3). You can also adjust settings like size, rotation etc. Then click on the green 'Save' tick, and click 'Add a new page'.

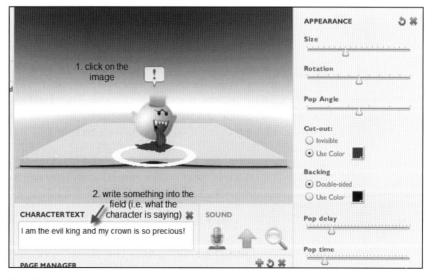

3: add text for characters

Top Tip 1: You can drag and drop your characters anywhere you want to by clicking on them and dragging them to a place you want.

Top Tip 2: If you want to add a character text, click on the image/character. If you wish to add narration, click on any other place, e.g. the page of the book.

8   Add as many pages as you wish.

9   After you have finished your story, click 'Save' in the top right corner.

10 When the Save is completed, click on 'My books' at the top of the page.

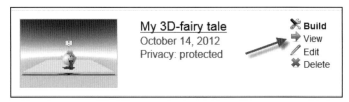

4: start the 3D-flipbook

12 Watch your 3D-flipbook by clicking on the blue arrows on the right. In order to see what the character is saying, click on '!' (see Image 5).

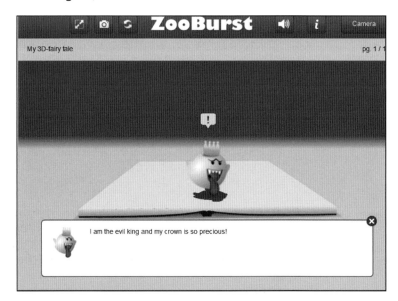

5: watching the story

13 In order to share the flipbook with others, click 'Share' and copy the URL (see Image 6).

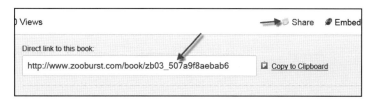

6: sharing the flipbook

in class

Lead-in

1   Put up some flashcards (or project some images) with pictures of prominent fairytale vocab (e.g. *princess*, *king*, *throne*, *wood*, *sword*, *hero* etc.).

2   Let students guess the words and write them below the flashcards (or, if you are using an interactive whiteboard or a screen and a projector, write or type them below the pictures).

3   Then, as a class, try to find adjectives that match the flashcards (e.g. *pretty princess*, *handsome prince*, *strict king* etc.). Write them on the board as well. The result will be a picture dictionary with typical fairytale phrases (adjective+noun).

4   Tell your students to carefully study the picture dictionary for 2 minutes.

5   Then turn the image so that only you can see it, and tell the students to relax and close their eyes.

6   Tell them that you are going to read out the words from the picture dictionary and that they should just listen to your voice and imagine the words.

7   Read the words, varying your voice appropriately to make the activity more interesting for the kids. Then tell your students that you are going to read the words again (this time with pauses) and that they should listen carefully and repeat the words.

8   Then tell your students to open their eyes again. Ask for volunteers who can list as many words as possible. When they list the words they can remember, hold up your fingers in a visible counting system, to help motivate them.

Online

1   Show your 3D-flipbook to your students.

2   Tell them that they are going to produce a similar flipbook.

3   Tell your students to register at www.zooburst.com, and help them with the registration process.

4   Show your students how to work with Zooburst.

5   Give your students plenty of time to create their own stories.

6   Walk around in class and help your students.

Follow-up

1   In the next lesson, let students present their stories.

2   In order for students to practise text writing, let them write a sequel to the fairy tale as homework.

Additional feature
Students can comment on their classmates' flipbooks; tell them to share the URL of their story and let them comment on it (see Image 7).

7: adding comments

Variation – Picture dictionary
This tool has good potential for your students to create mini-dictionaries or glossaries. They can use clipart from the site or from Google or FlickR, and add text. The 'dictionaries' can be projected on a screen and the words can be checked/tested/reviewed by clicking on '!'.

Learn more
http://zooburst.com/zb_gallery.php

Let's write a Twitter story!

Application:	Twitter, www.twitter.com; a microblogging service that allows users to send text-based posts of not more than 140 characters.
Focus:	writing short messages (140 characters) in a community, microblogging
Level:	pre-intermediate–advanced
Age:	under 13s may not sign up to Twitter, nor use it at all except via a Classroom Twitter Account set up by a teacher
Time:	60–90 minutes
ICT skills:	browsing, typing, copying & pasting
Equipment:	computer lab OR single computer, projector

Do It Yourself

1 Register for a Classroom Twitter Account at www.twitter.com. Try to think of a username for yourself that's easily memorable for your students.

   Note: If you don't like the idea of Twitter and tweeting, it might be the name itself, 'Twitter', that you don't like – a lot of people don't! You might feel more comfortable with it if you thought of it instead as a super-speedy and efficient messaging/information service.

2 Read the Twitter Basics below, and work through any relevant tutorials on our website's Twitter section.

3 For a good video introduction to Twitter, search for 'Twitter in Plain English' on YouTube.

You might like to reproduce these Twitter Basics for your students:

Twitter Basics
Note: for beginner and advanced tutorials, check YouTube: 'how to use Twitter'.
- *Twitter* is the application, and a *tweet* is the message you post, so you *tweet* a message.
- First, go to your profile page and upload a picture of yourself or, if you like, an avatar (a substitute image, if you don't want your own face to be shown publicly). To do this, click on he settings wheel in the top right corner, then 'Setting', then 'Profile', and upload a picture.
- Edit your profile by typing a short bio of yourself into the 'Bio' field.

- You can add other information about yourself if you choose. Remember, though, to be sensible about what personal information you give away to the world.
- To post a message, click on 'Home' in the top left corner, and then type your message into the 'Compose new Tweet' field (see Image 1).

1: the 'Compose new Tweet' field

- If you are looking for tweets by a certain person, click on the '#Discover' tab at the top of the page (see Image 2), then click on 'Find friends', and then type their name into the 'Search' field at the top right.

Note: You can also search for certain terms (*Web 2.0* etc.).

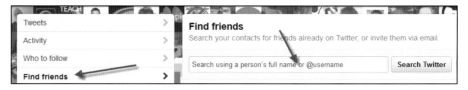

2: the Find friends search field

- If you want to set up the system so that it displays that person's tweets on your Home page whenever they make them, click 'Follow'.
- A list of tweets written by the people you are following is on the Home page, in the right-hand Tweets field. The order has the most recent at the top.
- To reply to a message, click on the Reply link, and below the name, type your message; although your message is mainly intended for @username, all your followers can read it too.
- In your message, you might like to use a # (in Twitter it's called a hashtag). This is very useful when you want to read more tweets about something in your message. E.g.: *Watching Austria vs. Germany tonight #euroqualifiers*. Once you've typed *'#euroqualifiers'* into the search box, all the messages that people in the whole Twitter community have posted about euroqualifiers will appear in your list.

- If you want to send a private message to a particular follower, use the Direct Message (DM) system. To do this, in the black bar at the very top of the page just to the right of the Search field is a wheel icon (settings). Click on that, and from the dropdown menu click Direct message, then New message, then complete the fields.
  NB You can't send a DM to someone you're following, but only to someone who's following you.
- 'Retweet' means forwarding a message that you like to your followers. Click on the 'Retweet' button.
- Favourites: if you like a certain tweet (containing, e.g., a useful link), you can add this message to your favourites. Click on the message, then click 'Favorite' to save it.
- To shorten URLs, programs like www.bit.ly will help.
- Once you've become familiar with Twitter, you might like to start tweeting yourself. On the Home page, at top left beneath your photo, see 'Compose new Tweet'.
- Also on the Home page beneath your photo is 'Following', which is the people you're following' and 'Followers', the people following you.

Top Tip (credit: Mark Brumley @markbrumley). To be ready for Online Step 8, decide on a unique hashtag to use for your class, such as *#fairy_tale_4b*.

in class

Lead-in

1 Ask your students whether or not they know about Twitter.

2 Ask those who do to come up with a simple explanation.

Then you can give them more information; here is a Wikipedia definition of Twitter:

Twitter is an online social networking service and microblogging service that enables its users to send and read text-based posts of up to 140 characters, known as "tweets". It was created in March 2006 by Jack Dorsey and launched that July. The service rapidly gained worldwide popularity, with over 300 million users as of 2011, generating over 300 million tweets and handling over 1.6 billion search queries per day. It has been described as "the SMS of the Internet". Twitter Inc. is based in San Francisco, with additional servers and offices in New York City.

3 Also discuss the etymological features of Twitter, e.g. 'tweet' (the sound a bird makes, hence a very short, precise message).

4 Then show the YouTube video: 'Twitter in plain English'.

5.5 Let's write a Twitter story!

Online

1   In the computer lab, show your students how to create a Twitter account.

2   Also give them a brief tutorial on how to work with Twitter (use Twitter Basics, in Do It Yourself 2).

3   Explain the purpose of a hashtag (#) in Twitter (Twitter Basics).

4   Start a story on Twitter with a maximum of 140 characters. Give your tweet a hashtag, so that the other students can easily track the story, e.g. in Class 4b it could be *#Timothystory4b*. Start a tweet like this: 'I know a boy. His name is Timothy. He loves pizza and mangoes. #twitterstory4b'.

5   Tell your students to continue the story, always adding the hashtag.

6   Give your students time to write. You can follow the story when you type *#twitterstory4b* into the search query.

    Note: we recommend that in bigger classes you set up groups of 4-6 students and have each group write their own story (using a different hashtag, e.g. *#twitterstory4b_1*, *#twitterstory4b_2* etc.). That way all the students get a chance to be more involved.

7   Then, they may want to share their stories, which can be displayed on a screen and you can point at the language generated.

8   Then tell your students to go to http://tweetchat.com/room/*#fairy_tale_4b* (i.e. the hashtag you generated in Do It Yourself 3). Tweetchat displays all the tweets from a hashtag; project Tweetchat onto the wall.

Variation 1 – A vocab a day
Try to think of a hashtag specifically for your class, e.g. *#english2csmith*. Post a new vocabulary word every day. Students should use this word, posting it in a meaningful, contextualised sentence. *Remind them to use the hashtag!*

Variation 2 – Twitter glossary
Allocate a hashtag to each unit in the textbook (e.g. #pollution_4b) – students have to provide a definition of certain words in it, using under 140 characters for each definition.

Variation 3 – Trivia madness!
Ask trivia questions on a certain topic relevant to your lessons. Students should post the answer in full sentences. Do not forget your class hashtag! e.g. *#english2csmith.*

Variation 4 – Twitpoll
Start a poll using Twitter. Polling is ideal if you want your students to post their opinions, points of view etc.

Variation 5 – Learning diary
For more mature students, you can use Twitter as a learning diary. Ask students to post their learning efforts, progress, difficulties, successes etc. *Remind them to add a hashtag!*

Variation 6 – Collaborative research
Post a useful link for your students on a certain topic you are dealing with at the moment. Tell your students that they have to find a relevant link as well, and share it with the community. *Remind them to add a hashtag!*

Variation 7 – 'It's quality that counts, not quantity'
Tell students to read an article/book etc. They should come up with a Twitter summary or even review (140 characters). *Remind them to add a hashtag!*

Variation 8 – Round table
Have a Twitter discussion with your students about an EFL-relevant topic. *Remind them to add a hashtag!*

Variation 9 – Translation tweet
Provide a sentence in your mother tongue and tell students to translate it into English. You can also provide a sentence in English for students to translate into their mother tongue. *Remind them to add a hashtag!*

Credits to: Prof. Steve Wheeler, http://steve-wheeler.blogspot.com/

5.6 Can you doo Toondoo?

Application: Toondoo, www.toondoo.com; lets you and your students create very appealing cartoons in a very short time.

Similar applications: Toonlet, www.toonlet.com; WittyComics, www.wittycomics.com; Pixton, www.pixton.com (for schools!)

Focus: creating cartoons

Level: all levels

Age: 13+ only; see Do It Yourself 1

Time: 60–80 minutes

ICT skills: browsing, typing, copying & pasting, uploading

Equipment: computer lab OR single computer, pictures of cartoon characters, projector

Do It Yourself

1 Sign up for a free individual account at www.toondoo.com. For full information about the age restriction, see http://www.toondoo.com/privacypolicy.jsp.

2 Click 'Toons' in the left top control bar, then from the dropdown menu, 'Create Toon' (see Image 1).

1: creating a Toon

3   Then choose the three-frame horizontal layout (you may find that loading this takes a few minutes).

4   In the top control bar you can choose characters (see Image 2), settings, speech bubbles etc.

2: choosing a character

5   Pick a character you like and drag it into the frame (see Image 3). To put a second character in the same frame, repeat the procedure.

3: dragging your character into the frame

6   Now you can add scenery, speech bubbles etc. by dragging them into the frame. Click on the top control bar, select one of the options that pop up below it, and drag it into your frame (see Image 4).

4: maximising speech bubbles

To minimise/maximise/flip/rotate speech bubbles, characters etc, use the bottom control bar (see Image 4 again).

Top Tip 1: If you want to copy an image into the next frame, click on the little box just above the frame (see Image 5).

5: copying the contents of one frame into the next

7   When you have finished your frames, click on the Main Menu tab and click 'Save' (see Image 6). Give your toon a title and description, then scroll down to click on 'Keep it Private!', undo 'let others redoo' and 'allow others to purchase this toon', and then go back up again to click on 'Publish'.

6: saving

8   Go back to www.toondoo.com On the home page click 'Books > Create Books'.

9   Now drag one of the frames you created into the book (see Image 7).

Note: vertical frames cannot be dragged into the book.

5.6 Can you doo Toondoo?

7: dragging a frame into your book

10 Then start to drag another set of frames upwards. As you do so,
the picture will change to let you insert frames before or after
the set you've just inserted (see Image 8). Drag your set into the
'Insert after this page' field. Click 'Publish' and give your book a
title. Then click 'View it now'.

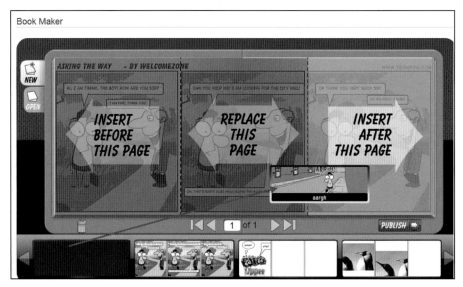

8: dragging another set of frames into a new page in your book

11 To save this cartoon to show to your students later, copy the URL.

5.6 Can you doo Toondoo?

Lead-in

1 Put some images of well-known cartoon characters such as Homer Simpson, Popeye, the Powerpuff Girls, onto the board. Elicit more names from your students and write them down on the board (if you have an IWB/a projector and internet connection, you may look for the pictures and place them on the board as well). You can ask the following questions:
   - Who are they?
   - What is the name of their cartoon?
   - What makes them so special/famous/popular?
   - What are their character traits?
   - Why are cartoons so popular?
   - Which cartoons do you read/watch? Why?
   - What makes a good cartoon?

Online

1 Show your cartoon to the students. Tell them that you are going to produce one as well.

2 Show them how to create a cartoon with Toondoo.

3 After your tutorial, let students form groups (depending on number of students and computers).

4 Depending on the level, they should produce a cartoon based on a certain text type/topic you did in class. Possible text types are:
   - Action story
   - Fairy tale
   - Interview
   - Detective story
   - Vampire story
   - Satirical cartoon.

5 Walk around in the lab and help your students with technical and linguistic questions.

6 After your students have finished, let them present their stories by presenting them on a projector.

   Top Tip 1: You can also tell your students to post their links on a backchannelling application like Todaysmeet or Wallwisher (see Activities 3.4 and 3.8).

   Top Tip 2: Your students can give feedback on their classmates' cartoons by visiting their URLs and posting a comment. They could give feedback on:
   - Layout
   - Plot

- Language
- Creativity.

Top Tip 3: If you do not have enough time in the computer lab, let students finish the cartoon at home; it's important that students get the idea of how Toondoo works.

Variation – Target vocab

These cartoons can be helpful for practising target vocabulary. For instance, at beginner level, students can create comics with common greeting expressions and phrases. At more advanced levels, you could provide specific vocabulary, language chunks and idioms, and ask your students to create comics that include the target lexis.

5.7 Anchorwoman style

Application: Cueprompter, www.cueprompter.com; an online teleprompter similar to those used in TV studios.

Focus: reading/writing an EFL text with a teleprompter

Level: intermediate–advanced

Age: any

Time: 50 minutes

ICT skills: browsing, typing, copying & pasting

Equipment: projector, laptop, computer lab; optional, pen drive for each student, video camera or smartphone

Preparation: For Lead-in Step 1, find a video recording of a typical news announcement (about a minute long) on any topic. Useful sources include: http://edition.cnn.com/video, http://news.sky.com/home/video, http://www.euronews.net/ ('last bulletin as video on demand').

Do It Yourself

1   Go to www. cueprompter.com. No registration is needed.

2   In the Quick start box, type (or paste) a script suitable for a newscast, change the screen size etc to your preferences and click 'Start Prompter' (see Image 1).

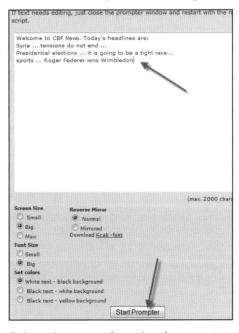

1: inserting text and starting the prompter

3   Your text will appear in a new window, ready to use as a teleprompter. To make it scroll up slowly, click 'Forward' at the top. You can adjust the scroll speed at the top as well; see Image 2. **Note:** If you want to go back to the beginning of the news text, click 'PgUp' (Image 2).

2: adjusting the scroll speed

Lead-in

1   Play your news announcement to your students.

2   Ask the following questions:
    * What was the news reporter talking about?
    * Were you able to understand everything?
    * What was the news reporter wearing?
    * What variety of English did you hear? (American, British, Australian etc.) How do you know?
    * What did you think about his/her language (speed, vocabulary, pronunciation?
    * Did you notice that he/she was reading from a script?

3   The last question leads on to your true intention: making your students aware that most news reporters read from a teleprompter (some of your students may already know this).

Online

1   Tell your students that they are going to be news announcers.

2   Tell your students to prepare a one-minute newscast about a topic you want them to practise (e.g. for higher levels, the Arab Revolution, or for lower levels a sports report).

3   Let your students do this task in pairs, both working as news announcers; they should each write a script for their newscast. Tell them that they can watch other videos and do additional research on the internet in order to study how news reporters behave. Tell them that some of them will be reading their scripts out to the class and, when they do this, they should try to imitate (gestures, typical phrases, intonation, etc.) the performance of the news announcer they watched before in the video. If necessary, you can play the video again and discuss striking features in class. Walk around in class and help your students draft their scripts.

4   After your students have finished drafting their scripts, tell them to save them on their pen drive/flash drive/USB stick and hand these to you. (If your students do not have pen drives, ask them to email their text to you – or, if all else fails, ask them to write their scripts on a sheet of paper and hand them to you. You will need to type their texts into the Quick Start window. Unless you can set your students a task to keep them busy while you're typing, it would be better to stop the lesson at this point and start another lesson when you've done the typing.)

5   Choose a script and go to http://cueprompter.com, using a single laptop which will then become the teleprompter.

6   Paste the text from the pen drive into the surface and click 'Start Prompter'. Now the laptop is a teleprompter.

7   Now, ask the two students who wrote the script to come to the front and sit down on a chair with a table (imitating a news room). Place the laptop in front of them.

8   Now tell your students that they should each read their script acting like a news announcer. Start the teleprompter by clicking 'Forward', and adjust the speed as necessary.

9   You can repeat this procedure (depending on time) with several other pairs.

   Top Tip 1: If your students do not mind, you can videotape them (with a camera or your mobile phone) and discuss their performance as a class.

   Top Tip 2: In order to make the scene as authentic as possible, you can ask your kids to dress up for next time (suits, dresses). You can also use the board as the background of the news room (put up poster, draw images typical of a newsroom, e.g. the world etc.).

Top Tip 3: If you do not have enough time to let all of your students present, tell them to prepare their script and presentation at home (i.e. they use their own computer as the teleprompter and record themselves with their smartphones, webcams etc.). Of course, they can also dress up at home. In the next lesson they should present their broadcasts.

Top Tip 4: To record themselves doing the newscast, they could use internet-based sites such as MailVU, (see Activity 1.6); they can open two internet tabs (one for Cueprompter, one for MailVU). They start recording on MailVU and then start playing the prompter and speaking. When done, they stop the video recording. If you wanted to play this in class next time and give feedback, you could copy the URL generated into MailVU.

Variation 1 – *It's hard to be the president*

When discussing controversial topics in the EFL lesson (e.g. pollution, mass tourism, drug trafficking, violent computer games etc.) use Cueprompter for a role play. Tell your students that they are the president of the USA who has to give a TV speech to the nation about a controversial topic, clearly expressing her/his point of view. Tell them to include all the arguments you were discussing in class, or they can use a computer to do some research on the internet. Tell them to prepare a three-minute speech considering the following things:

- Introduction (greetings, why the president is addressing the nation)
- Arguments for/against the topic using phrases expressing your point of view (*I think, I truly believe that, I am of the opinion, I want to emphasise* etc.)
- Conclusion (summing-up arguments, greetings)

Variation 2 – *Casting time*

Tell your students that they are going to take part in a casting for a radio reporter. Prepare a radio news announcement (copy from the internet) and paste it into Cueprompter. Now your students have to read this text without making a mistake. Pretend to be a strict broadcaster, and dismiss the students if they make a mistake.

Note: It is important not to humiliate students making mistakes – it is more about the fun of competition.

Useful Resources

Web 2.0, New Learning Technologies (and EFL)

http://www.freetech4teachers.com/
Free Technology for Teachers;
free resources and lesson plans for teaching with technology
written by Richard Byrne.

http://nikpeachey.blogspot.com/
Nik's Learning Technology blog by Nik Peachey, for English
Language teachers.

http://edtechtoolbox.blogspot.com
EdTech Toolbox: a place to share e-learning and Web 2.0 tools for
education.
Computers and laptops in education are important only when
used with good pedagogy. Digital content and creation is an
important part of the process for educators in the 21st century.

http://usingictinfe.blogspot.com/
Using ICT in further education; free resources for teachers and
students (Open Source, Freeware, Creative Commons); Patricia
Donaghy.

http://lifefeast.blogspot.com/
Ana María Menzes blogging on new media.

http://quickshout.blogspot.com/
Nik's QuickShout; educational technology and ELT.

http://coolcatteacher.blogspot.com/
Cool Cat teacher blog; teaching students with new tools,
enthusiasm, and the belief that teaching is a noble calling, by
Vicki Davis.

http://www.markbrumley.com/
Mark Brumley: educational technology.

http://ozgekaraoglu.edublogs.org/
Ozge Karaoglu's blog about teaching, learning, reflecting and
being a 21st-century learner and teacher.

http://teachertrainingvideos.com/
Teacher training videos by Russell Stannard.

http://www.commoncraft.com/
The CommonCraft Show by Lee Lefeever.

Useful Resources

http://theedublogger.com/
The Edublogger: tips and tricks for educators.
http://cyber-kap.blogspot.com/
Technology Tidbits: Thoughts of a Cyber Hero, by David Kapuler.

http://www.mguhlin.org/
Around the Corner; MGuhlin.org.

http://www.ictineducation.org/
ICT in Education; educational technology.

http://techtipsforteachersblog.blogspot.com/
Tech tips for teachers.

http://www.learning-reloaded.com
Learning with new technologies. Thomas Strasser.

http://www.livebinders.com/play/play_or_edit?id=26329
Web 2.0 tools. Suzie Vesper.

http://cooltoolsforschools.wikispaces.com/
Web 2.0-tools collection.

http://technology4kids.pbworks.com/w/page/24292734/
FrontPage
Great collection using new technologies with kids; Shelly S. Terrell.

http://www.scoop.it/t/web-2-0-tools-for-language-learning
Web 2.0 for language learning. Vicky Saumell.

http://www.classroom20.com/
Web 2.0 in the classroom. Steve Hargadon.

http://edtech-hub.blogspot.co.at/
Tools for teaching with technology.

http://larryferlazzo.edublogs.org/2010/06/28/my-best-posts-for-tech-novices-plus-one-from-somebody-else/
Posts for tech novices. Larry Ferlazzo.

http://fremdsprachenundneuemedien.blogspot.com/
Jürgen Wagner's blog and links on teaching English with new media.

TEFL in general

http://www.breakingnewsenglish.com
Sean Banville: Free, 13-Page, Ready-to-Print EFL/ESL Lesson Plans on Current Events.
http://jeffreyhill.typepad.com

Jeffrey Hill: The English Blog: internet resources, reviews, news, tips and trivia for learners and teachers of English.

http://www.jochenenglish.de
Jochen English: blog by Jochen Lüders (München).

http://daily-english-activities.*blogspot*.com
Nik's Daily English Activities | For English language and digital literacy skills.

http://www.elementalenglish.com
Elemental English: teaching the English of everyday life.

http://efllecturer.blogspot.com
The Lecturer's EFL SMART blog: EFL, ESL and ESOL learning activities for smart students of English.

http://random-idea-english.blogspot.com
Random Idea English: a mishmash of lessons, exercises and the occasional opinionated rant about the English language.

http://efl-resource.com
TEFL resources and lesson ideas.

http://eslclassroomactivities.wordpress.com
ESL classroom activities and more.

http://rosa58.blogspot.com
English all over.

http://www.wagner-juergen.de/englisch/
A site written mostly in German, but which has a great collection of EFL links.

http://www.bbc.co.uk/worldservice/learningenglish/
BBC English learning site.

http://learnenglish.britishcouncil.org/en/
Learning English, British Council.

Useful Resources

http://learnenglishkids.britishcouncil.org/en/
Learning English Kids British council.

http://www.teachingenglish.org.uk/
British Council Teaching English.

http://www.eslcafe.com/
An extensive collection of exercises.

http://www.onestopenglish.com
Many exercises for TEFL teachers.

http://www.eslbase.com/
A nice choice of activities.

http://larryferlazzo.edublogs.org/
Websites of the day for EFL teachers. Larry Ferlazzo.

http://community.eflclassroom.com/
EFL material.

credits: Jürgen Wagner (@wagjuer) and Daniel Martín.

Quick reference guide

This guide will help you select an activity suitable for your class based on the time you have available, the learning level(s) of your students and the CLIL and language elements.

To use it, look down the left-hand columns until you come to an activity suitable for your students' language level and age, then look across to see the app name and focus, lesson time and page number. Or, if you prefer, first look for the focus you would like to cover or the time you have available (the activities are listed in order of increasing time).

Please note that the guidance is very basic; it allows you to see the approximate language level of an activity when you are doing it plus the time it is likely to take; you are free to change the timing of any activity or expand it as you wish.

A1 BEGINNER	A2 ELEMENTARY	B1 PRE-INTERMEDIATE	B1 INTERMEDIATE	B2 UPPER INTERMEDIATE	C1 ADVANCED	AGE	APP	FOCUS	LESSON TIME (MINS)	PAGE NO
Chapter 1 – Teacher tools										
		1 Show you know! (variation)				13+	Learning Apps	create online quizzes	15–30	18
		2 Share the good work (variation)				13+	Authorstream	sharing Powerpoint presentations on the web	10	22
		3 Tube this – tube that …				none	Quietube	watch YouTube videos without any onscreen distractions	0	24
		4 My YouTube Channel				none	YouTube	create YouTube playlists, retrieve videos easily	0	26
			5 Tool time … (variation)			none	Classtools	create educational games, activities	10–60	29
		6 Hey, teacher, tell me what to do! (variation)				none	mailVU	create video emails or messages	5+	32
Chapter 2 – Visualisation										
				1 'I have a dream'		none	Wordle	interpreting and creating visual input	30–40	36
			2 'Let's do the time warp again'			13+	Capzles	creating timelines of events	60	42
			3 Vocab visualiser			none	PhasR	visualising written sentences	30	47
				4 Glogster it!		< 13, parental permission	Glogster	creating interactive desktop	variable	50
				5 Photostory 2.0		13+	Photovisi	creating photo stories	60	58
		6 Tune my handout!				none	Signgenerator	embedding graphics into handouts etc	variable	62
		7 Arty stories				<18, parental approval	Storybird	creating picture stories	60	65
		8 Prezi for Prezident!				none	Prezi	creating dynamic, non-linear presentations	variable	69
			9 Been there, done that …			13+	Tripline	reconstructing trips on Google Maps	90	74
			10 Ka-ching!			none	Wordsift	creating tag clouds, sentences and thesaurus	50	80

A1 BEGINNER	A2 ELEMENTARY	B1 PRE-INTERMEDIATE	B1 INTERMEDIATE	B2 UPPER INTERMEDIATE	C1 ADVANCED	AGE RESTRICTIONS	APP	FOCUS	LESSON TIME (MINS)	PAGE NO
		11 Australia is QReat!				none	GoQR	creating QR codes	30	84
		12 Funky Pic Dic style				<13 must use your educator account	Animoto	creating multimedia presentations	20	89
		13 Show me what you like!				13+	Screenr	producing screencasts	60	94
Chapter 3 – Collaboration										
			1 'Once upon a time …'			none	PiratePad	collaborative text writing in real time	30	100
				2 Webpage juror		none	Markup	webpage analysis	40+	105
				3 Chief analyst		none, or 13+ to register	Crocodoc	collaboratively work on online texts	60	111
			4 Backchannelling			13+	Todaysmeet	posting questions during lessons	variable	114
			5 Go vote!			none	Flisti	creating a poll	10	118
				6 Brainstorming deluxe		13+	Popplet	interactive and collaborative mindmapping	60–90	121
				7 My thoughts 2.0		< 13, parental permission	Voicethread	collaborative brainstorming using text, image and speech	45	126
			8 Another stick in the wall			none	Wallwisher	collaborative mindmapping with sticky notes	30	131
			9 I need a hand …			none	Tricider	creating simple decision-making process	10–15	135
Chapter 4 – Audio										
	1 Do you speak … Voki?					none, or 13+ to register	Voki	making animated text/speech	60	140
	2 'Listen up! That's me!'					13+; <18 need parental permission	Audioboo	creating audio files from speech	60	147
		3 Voice upon a time …				best for 3-14	Little Bird Tales	creating audio tales	60–120	151
				4 'This is school radio!'		13+	Spreaker	producing radio shows/podcasts	120	157

Chapter 5 – Writing

A1 BEGINNER	A2 ELEMENTARY	B1 PRE-INTERMEDIATE	B1 INTERMEDIATE	B2 UPPER INTERMEDIATE	C1 ADVANCED	AGE RESTRICTIONS	APP	FOCUS	LESSON TIME (MINS)	PAGE NO
			1 My online book project			none	Livebinders	presenting work online	variable	164
	2 My flipbook story					13+	Flipsnack	embedding texts into flipbooks	50	170
				3 Things I learnt today		13+; <18 need parental permission	Penzu	creating a personal online diary	10	174
	4 Can you see? - it's 3D!					none	Zooburst	creating 3D flipbook stories	60	177
			5 Let's write a Twitter story!			none, if using classroom account	Twitter	writing short messages/ microblogging	60–90	183
		6 Can you doo Toondoo?				13+	Toondoo	creating cartoons	60-80	188
				7 Anchorwoman style		none	Cueprompter	using a teleprompter	50	195